Is Everybody Ready for Kindergarten?

Is Everybody Ready for Kindergarten?

A Tool Kit for Preparing Children and Families

ANGÈLE SANCHO PASSE

Redleaf Press®
www.redleafpress.org
800-423-8309

Published by Redleaf Press
10 Yorkton Court
St. Paul, MN 55117
www.redleafpress.org

First edition 2010
Cover design by Jim Handrigan
Interior typeset in Minion Pro and designed by Erin New
Printed in the United States of America

17   16   15   14   13   12   11   10   1   2   3   4   5   6   7   8

Library of Congress Cataloging-in-Publication Data

Passe, Angèle Sancho.
    Is everybody ready for kindergarten? : a tool kit for preparing children
and families / Angèle Sancho Passe.
        p. cm.
    Includes bibliographical references.
    ISBN 978-1-60554-015-3 (alk. paper)
 1. Kindergarten. 2. Kindergarten—Parent participation. I. Title.
    LB1167.P37 2010
    372.21'9—dc22

                                    2010003750

Printed on FSC-certified paper

Mixed Sources
Product group from well-managed
forests and other controlled sources
www.fsc.org Cert no. SW-COC-002283
© 1996 Forest Stewardship Council

FSC

To all the children getting ready for

kindergarten together with their parents,

care providers, and teachers

Contents

Acknowledgments

Writing this book has been even more fun than I thought it would be. I enjoyed the solo work of sorting relevant research, hunting for words, and crafting sentences and paragraphs to make the content understandable and useful. I also loved the collaborative process of exchanging ideas, getting feedback, and receiving support. I am very grateful to many generous people who contributed so much in these intense months.

First, thank you to the children, parents, teachers, and providers who allowed me to observe and ask questions. They gave me great advice about how to make the transition to kindergarten better.

To Jim, my husband, for his warm and steady encouragement and that first cup of fresh coffee on the days that needed to start slow after a late night of writing.

To Oliver, my son, for his insightful critique of the first manuscript, during Christmas vacation—a most precious holiday present.

To Alexia, my daughter, for her well-timed "How's the book coming?" and her attentive listening.

To Jeanine, my mother, for her continuing pride in her former kinder-gartner.

To Marietta Rice and Beth Cutting, dear friends and early childhood and family education experts, for asking all the right questions at the beginning, during an invigorating fall weekend at the cabin.

To Kate Horst, Kathy Lathrop, and Sheryl Warner, colleagues and leaders in early childhood care and education, for their thoughtful reading of chapters and knowledgeable suggestions.

To Maureen Seiwert, executive director of early childhood education in the Minneapolis public schools, for the opportunity to contribute to the transition to kindergarten in her programs.

To Betty Cooke, for sharing historical perspectives and for her leadership in developing early learning standards in Minnesota.

To David Heath and Kyra Ostendorf at Redleaf Press for their trust in me and in this project.

To Jennifer Shepard and Laurie Herrmann, my editors, for their straightforward and comforting partnership.

And, of course, to all my colleagues, friends, and family members, too numerous to list by name, who took an interest in and periodically asked about the book or gave me encouragement and confidence.

Introduction

My first day of kindergarten was on a bright day in January 1956 in Oran, Algeria. Despite the warmth of the North African winter sun shining on the school courtyard, I remember being cold. It was not a pleasant experience. I could see my mother's teary eyes as my new kindergarten teacher sternly told her to leave quickly. I was a smart little girl and eager to learn, but throughout that first year of school, it became obvious that Madame D did not approve of my learning style or my mother's parenting style, so she dourly predicted neither one of us would go far in life! We were glad for the June siroccos, the hot desert winds that signaled the beginning of summer vacation.

My own children started kindergarten in 1977 and 1980 at Marcy Open School in Minneapolis. They both had Greg as their kindergarten teacher. He was a wonderful educator, blending personal warmth and outstanding teaching skills to launch his young students' academic careers. Greg was famous for his teddy bear parades, as well as for making stone soup and pulling loose teeth, an important rite of passage for five- and six-year-olds. When I volunteered in his classroom, I learned what an excellent kindergarten should look and feel like. This kindergarten was both developmentally appropriate *and* academically challenging. My children's positive experiences made up for my own experience of kindergarten.

In the 1980s and early 1990s, as an early childhood teacher and parent educator in the Minneapolis public schools, I designed several transition-to-kindergarten projects, the most successful model being a workshop called "It's Time to Think about Kindergarten." During three evenings, the workshop includes the topics "Choosing a School," tips for picking a school; "Your Child's Experience in Kindergarten," tips for understanding what children do and learn in kindergarten; and "Your Experience as the Parent of a Kindergartner," options for family involvement. The sessions were offered to families with a child who would soon enter school. They could attend as many sessions as they wanted. An elementary school and the community education department cosponsored the program, and it was free to parents, who came to learn about how to prepare their child and themselves for this new experience. One of the kindergarten teachers hosted the group in his classroom, which was always a big hit as parents could visualize their child learning in that setting.

In the mid and late 1990s, as a district administrator, I maintained my focus on the transition to kindergarten by leading the School Readiness Collaborative. Part of my job was to work with community and district early childhood programs to ensure they implemented quality preschool services. I also worked with elementary schools to design transition-to-kindergarten activities.

As an educational consultant since 2000, I have continued to think about the transition to kindergarten while designing curriculum, writing articles, conducting studies, facilitating focus groups, and training educators at local and national conferences. It's fair to say that the transition to kindergarten from the point of view of children, families, preschool programs, and elementary schools has been on my mind, personally and professionally, for a long time. I have learned a lot in the process and will share that with you in this book.

Malika is standing in front of me, her brown eyes sparkling and her hands on her hips. "You know what? After I'm five, I am going to kindergarten!"

"You are? And what is that?" I ask.

"That's the big school, silly!" She rolls her eyes, incredulous at my ignorance of life's important things. "For the big kids, because I am big now."

Malika's mom sighs. "Yes, my baby is a big kid now." She looks proud and a little apprehensive at the same time. Her face tells me that going to kindergarten will be a big event for this family, even though Malika is going to the neighborhood elementary school, which is only five blocks from her home and where her brother is already in the second grade.

Going to kindergarten is the official beginning of a child's educational career. It is an important part of child development and the family life cycle. It is also an important time for the school to make a good first impression. Similarly, I want to begin this book's important discussion by presenting my beliefs, which are based on current research, best practices, and my years of professional experience and observations.

- The transition to kindergarten is not a one-time event.

  A *transition* is a passage from one place or stage to another. It requires adapting feelings, thoughts, and behaviors from an old situation to a new one. When children enter kindergarten, they go from the intimate world of home or child care to the institutional world of education, especially if they attend a public school. Their families make the same adaptation. The transition is not a one-time event happening on the first day of school; rather, the transition begins before children enter school and continues during their first year. The family, the preschool program, and the receiving elementary school all play important roles in making the transition smooth and productive. In order for this to happen, these three groups must know one another well, understand their different roles, share information, express their hopes, and work together for the children's benefit (Pianta, Rimm-Kaufman, and Cox 1999).

- Going to kindergarten is a developmental milestone.

    Regardless of educational, cultural, or socioeconomic background, all families know about going to school, and all families want their children to do well in school. The entry into kindergarten is a milestone in the lives of families, likely the most important step since the child was born. Even for children who have attended a child care center or a family child care home, kindergarten is the beginning of their formal education. Starting kindergarten is exciting and scary at the same time. It can also be intimidating, particularly for families with lower levels of education and for new immigrants who are not familiar with the culture and language of education.

- All families want the best for their children.

    Depending on their level of education and knowledge of the educational system, families have different ways of viewing kindergarten. Highly educated families tend to approach the entrance to kindergarten in the same way they would approach looking for a college. They conduct research and visit schools to choose the one that best meets their needs. Parents feel confident in their ability to advocate for their child, so they ask about curriculum, visit the school's Web site to review test scores, and sign up to volunteer in the classroom.

    Immigrant families, families in poverty, and families with low educational levels are less familiar with the culture of education. These families are not as aware of their choices, and they may not know how to conduct the search. If their child already attends a preschool program, they rely on guidance from the staff. They also expect that the school system will help them and provide the best for their children. They are unsure about the rules and expectations schools have regarding family involvement. Unfortunately, if they act in ways that do not match educators' hopes, they are perceived as being uninterested in their children's education (Christenson 1999).

- Not all children have the same readiness for kindergarten.

   State and national studies estimate that about half of children do not have the skills needed to be successful in school. There is a wide difference in the experiences of children before they enter kindergarten. Children who participate in a quality preschool program (at a center or in family child care, public or private) are better prepared for school; however, about one-third of three- and four-year-old children in low-income families are enrolled in preschool, compared to about two-thirds of children in higher-income families (Olson 2007). At the same time, a child's home environment can either enhance or limit the child's opportunities for learning (Hart and Risley 1995, 1999).

   To be ready for kindergarten, five-year-old children should have the early literacy and social-emotional skills to take care of themselves. In addition to being reasonably healthy, they also should have the language to ask adults for what they need as well as the ability to play cooperatively with their classmates. School-ready five-year-olds should also understand and be able to do the new things they are learning academically. More children could be ready for kindergarten if their parents, caregivers, and early child-hood teachers would prepare them intentionally for kindergarten.

- Early childhood programs have a big role in the transition to kindergarten.

   Preschools, child care centers, family child care homes, Head Start, and early childhood curriculum in public schools are the programs *sending* children to kindergarten. They are usually familiar with the expectations of school readiness set by state or federal mandates, but they often feel disconnected from the expectations of the elementary schools in their community. They need to have as much information as possible about what happens in kindergarten classrooms. When there is a strong connection between the pre-K and the K-12 worlds, there are more opportunities to offer continuity for children and families (Pianta and Kraft-Sayre 2003).

- Schools must be ready for children and families.

    Even though kindergarten is not part of compulsory education in every state, in 2005 about three-quarters of children in the United States attended a half-day or full-day public kindergarten (Editorial Projects in Education 2007). Look at the big discount-store displays in August to realize the importance of schooling in our culture. Families view kindergarten as the official first year of school; yet, not all schools treat children and families in the same way. Some schools are warm and welcoming places, while others are cold and unwelcoming. The latter is particularly true for immigrant families, families of color, and families in poverty. In focus groups, these families complain about a lack of respect and worry that their children are not being accepted.

    Family involvement is at its highest in kindergarten and tends to decline thereafter. If they feel welcome and connected, families with kindergarteners are open and ready to develop loyalty to the school and the school district. For the school district, this first year is the most critical opportunity to engage families as partners in education. The maxim "There is only one time to make a good first impression" applies here. Rather than only asking parents to adapt to the rules and views of the school, it is important for the school to learn what families want and expect. This honors parents' hopes and dreams for their children and engages them positively as partners in education right from the beginning (Doucet and Tudge 2007).

- Coordination and planning make the transition to kindergarten easier.

    Families expect a smooth path from preschool to kindergarten. Not only is learning continuity for children important, but it is also the law for children in early childhood special education (Individuals with Disabilities Education Improvement Act 2004) and for children of low-income families (No Child Left Behind Act of 2001; Improving Head Start for School Readiness Act of

2007). School districts and communities need a transition-to-kindergarten plan to help children and parents enter kindergarten (Ramey and Ramey 1999). This plan needs to be based on current research and should be simple enough for busy staff to implement.

- A good transition to kindergarten benefits children, families, and schools.

   Families with children who are in early childhood special education tend to receive the most comprehensive transition-to-kindergarten planning. Staff from both the preschool and the elementary school write and implement the Individual Education Plan (IEP) with parents. This intense level of coordination may not be practical or necessary for all children; however, all children adapt faster and more easily when specific activities are designed to help them enter school. Parents who feel welcome and understand what is expected of them can support their children with more confidence. Teachers who get to know their children and families well are more likely to have high expectations of student performance (Melton, Limber, and Teague 1999). The long-term benefits of a strong family-school partnership are invaluable: stronger academic achievement, positive behavior, better attendance, fewer placements in special education, and higher post-secondary enrollment (Ramey and Ramey 1999).

- Kindergarten is the first step on the way to college.

   Education is valuable for all, but not everyone knows how to navigate its system. Currently only about one-third of adults in the United States have completed a bachelor's degree. Another one-third has some college education or a two-year degree (Olson 2007). These numbers are much lower for minority groups. If school districts across the country are designing plans that promise to prepare all students for a secondary education, what do we need to do to help our children go from kindergarten to college? I conducted focus groups with immigrant parents who were very preoccupied with this question. As the starting point to a school career, kindergarten is the first opportunity that paves the way for college.

Using This Book

This book contains information about children's transition to kindergarten as well as practical ideas and activities for children and parents and preschool, child care, and kindergarten staff. Based on your needs, you might use the entire book as a planning tool or use parts of it that are more relevant for your particular situation. The following list provides examples of how different people might apply what they read.

- Child care center directors or elementary school principals might find ideas for training staff on the transition to kindergarten.
- Family child care providers might use the vocabulary to explain school readiness to parents as well as for tips to give them on how to prepare their children for kindergarten.
- College instructors might include information in a syllabus to provide students with a comprehensive view of the transition to kindergarten.
- Parent educators might use the contents to prepare handouts for parent-child workshops.
- Preschool teachers might integrate the ideas into curricula for children preparing for kindergarten.
- Kindergarten teachers and preschool teachers might read the book together in a study group and develop a comprehensive transition-to-kindergarten plan.

- Community foundations that support a transition-to-kindergarten project might develop a one-day conference around the main topics covered in this book.

- Home visitors might find simple and fun activities to help child care providers and parents make the transition to kindergarten easier for their children.

Tools for Educators

When I present workshops to educators on the transition to kindergarten, I always begin by asking participants what they want to learn during their time with me. Their questions are usually very practical: What should we say to parents about school readiness? What are best practices for the transition to kindergarten? What are good ways to engage kindergarten teachers as partners? How do we help pre-K teachers better prepare children? How should we work with immigrant families who are new to our school system? What can the principal do to make the school more welcoming? What is school readiness?

Kindergarten used to be viewed as the rehearsal year for school, but it has become clear that kindergarten is a much more important time. As the early childhood field has evolved, professionals wonder if they're doing enough to prepare learners. My objective with *Is Everybody Ready for Kindergarten?* is to give educators the tools they need to prepare learners.

How the Book Is Organized

Even though the book is organized in a sequence, you can consult the parts in which you are most interested. Chapter 1 explores the concepts of children being ready for school, as well as schools being ready for children and families. Chapter 2 examines kindergarten in the twenty-first century. Chapter 3 describes the characteristics of four-, five-, and six-year-old children, helping educators and caregivers understand their development, and it includes activities to facilitate the transition from preschool to kindergarten. Chapter 4 addresses the hopes and concerns parents have about kindergarten and includes activities for helping parents become active partners in their child's education. Chapter 5 covers the role of preschools and other sending programs in facilitating the transition to kindergarten. Chapter 6 offers strategic planning tools to help you prepare for the transition to kindergarten.

At the end of each chapter, discussion starters help you think more deeply about the information you've read and find practical solutions for your own challenges. You can use the questions individually or in discussions with colleagues. There are also checklists and a template for you to use in your program or in training staff or parents. I want this book to be of practical use to you, so feel free to modify them for your own situation.

CHAPTER 1

Children Ready for School, Schools Ready for Children and Families

Omar is five years old. Today is his first day of school, and he is all dressed up for it. Last week he went with his mom to a discount store to get his school uniform—khaki pants and a dark-blue polo shirt. The Head Start program he attended since he was three years old gave him a Superman backpack as a graduation present. His grandparents bought him spiffy blue and white sneakers. His shiny black hair is neatly combed with a perfect part.

Is Omar ready for school? Is his school ready for him? School readiness goes both ways. Children need to be ready for school and schools need to be ready for children and families.

When the words *school readiness* are mentioned they often provoke tension, with a hint of exasperation. Someone resolve the issue of who should be the most ready, please! Everyone agrees with the concept, but the definition is not clearly articulated. At one point, the ability of children to tie their shoes was high on the school readiness list, but with the creation of new shoe designs, that skill is no longer as much of a priority. Preschool educators, family child care providers, kindergarten teachers, administrators, and parents all want clarification.

The Concept of School Readiness for Children

As he gets off the bus, Omar looks shyly at the jolly principal greeting the children: "Welcome to school, boys and girls. I know it's going to be a good year for everyone!" Omar follows the line into the building and goes to room 102. Ms. Annie, the kindergarten teacher, says hello to him and shows him where to hang his backpack. She says, "I am so happy you are in my class, Omar. I remember you and your mom from the school picnic last week!" Omar grins. "I see you to picnic!" Then Ms. Annie takes him to the sign-in table. She believes in establishing routines on the first day. Omar chooses the blue marker, his favorite color, and confidently writes O-m-a-r. He used to do this every day at Head Start, and his mom helped him continue to practice during the summer.

When all the children have arrived, Ms. Annie brings them together for circle time to sing the good-morning song, which is sung in English to the tune of "Frère Jacques." At the end, Ms. Annie says, "That was 'good morning' in English! Now we are going to say good morning in Spanish and Hmong, because some of you speak Spanish and Hmong at home too." Omar blurts out, "Buenos días!" Ms. Annie smiles and says, "Yes, let's all say 'Buenos días,' like Omar!"

Ms. Annie reads the book Look Out Kindergarten, Here I Come! *by Nancy Carlson, which is the same book Omar's Head Start teacher read last spring during the kindergarten theme. Omar listens with interest. He raises his hand when Ms. Annie asks the children if they feel the same as Henry, the main character, on this first day of school—a little bit scared and excited at the same time. At the end of the story, Ms. Annie shows the children the calendar. She leads them into counting to seven, since today is September 7. Omar counts along, concentrating on the numbers, moving his fingers. Is Omar ready for school?*

When I ask kindergarten teachers and principals what being ready for school means to them, they usually respond, "Just give me children who are well rested and fed, get along with others, take care of themselves, and know how to sit still, and I will teach them the academic skills they need." In private conversations and in national surveys, educators tend to focus on social and physical development as the most important aspects of school readiness (Meisels 1999). At the same time, research shows that children with poor language and literacy skills are at a big disadvantage when they enter school. For example, when children do not have a good vocabulary, they are not able to understand the books read to them (Tabors, Beals, and Weizman 2001). Further, if children are unable to understand the story, there may be little to hold their attention. If this is the cause of their inability to sit still at circle time, attempts at teaching them to be quiet and to sit cross-legged may not necessarily improve their behavior. The focus on behavior as the most critical measure of school readiness can become frustrating.

The School Readiness Road

The best approach to thinking about school readiness is to look at children in a holistic way (Copple and Bredekamp 2009). The *whole child* includes body, mind, and emotions. In educational terms, it means addressing physical, cognitive, and social-emotional development. We need to nurture development so children develop specific skills and behaviors, with the understanding that they will be *on the road* to school readiness. To help teachers and providers assess children's abilities, there are various comprehensive child observation checklists, such as the *Work Sampling System*, the *Creative Curriculum for Preschool* model, or the *Child Observation Record (COR)*, each of which has a reliable system for indicating overall child development.

The developmental perspective dictates that children will not achieve the same degree of school readiness at the exact same time, nor will they move at the same pace (Copple and Bredekamp 2009). Typically developing children will have the same skills and behaviors around the same chronological age. And the job of educators is to use developmentally appropriate practices to teach. In other words, educators need to offer activities that are meaningful, fun, and physically and mentally possible for the children to do. Educators also need to scaffold, or gently guide, children to the next step of learning—not too hard, not too easy, but just right.

I like to think about school readiness as being like a cross-country race where there is no mad sprinting but a steady, intentional pace. This analogy comes to mind because my daughter is an amateur long-distance runner, and my husband and I have watched her race many times. Picture the runners at the starting point. They have different body types, running styles, clothes, shoes, and warm-up techniques. They probably have had different training programs, diets, and advice from coaches. But there they all are, on a cloudy Sunday morning, at point A on the road to point Z, with several water stations for rest and rehydration along the way.

Watching the race, driving from station to station, we recognize many of the runners. We notice they have different levels of support. Some have coaches who run alongside. Others have relatives and friends on the side of the road who encourage them by calling their names. Others do not have direct supporters, but strangers, like me, who shout general praise: "Keep going. You are almost there. Good running, number 342!" Even though the racers are running at different speeds and with various forms, one rule is clear: all participants are going in the same direction toward the same point. A few reach the finish line well before those in the large pack, who arrive within a compact time frame, and a few pull in at the end. All the participants are proud to have finished, having accomplished so much!

It is reasonable to expect that all children will have the skills and behaviors to be ready for school (Bowman 2006). Doing well in school is necessary for success in life. Early educators can help children achieve success in a thoughtful way, like the coaches who run alongside the runners. Good education should not be one-size-fits-all, with only one teaching approach for all children, whether or not they learn. And it is important to avoid extremes. Good education should not be completely individualized either, waiting for children to learn on their own time. Thoughtful teachers scaffold children's learning by offering manageable challenges. It is unreasonable to show four-year-olds how to write their names once and expect them to do it on their own. It is also unreasonable to let them scribble randomly rather than give them repeated opportunities to practice forming the letters of their names and be successful in spelling their names.

Early Learning Standards and Indicators of Progress

Enough research-based information exists about what children should know. Thoughtful early childhood educators have developed national and international early learning standards and indicators of progress. For example, the Minnesota Department of Education created the *Early Childhood Indicators of Progress: Minnesota's Early Learning Standards* in 2005. Based on early education and child development research, this publication gives a comprehensive overview of what three-, four-, and five-year-olds need to know. The standards describe expectations of children in six domains: social and emotional development, approaches to learning, language and literacy, creativity and the arts, cognitive development, and physical and motor development. These areas complement each other and are critical for overall development. Since children grow at individual rates but in a predictable way, most children will meet the majority of expectations for developmental standards by the time they enter kindergarten. As of 2007, three-quarters of our states had established standards of learning for early childhood, some focusing mostly on language and literacy (Barnett et al. 2007). The emphasis on language is important, as many of the indicators can be mastered only with the help of good language skills.

Find out about your own state's development of early learning standards. The National Child Care Information and Technical Assistance Center (NCCIC), a national resource center for information on child care, has a very comprehensive Web site (www.nccic.acf.hhs.gov) that allows you to search by state or territory and find out what is happening with early learning standards in your area.

The Minnesota Department of Education and Minnesota Department of Human Services developed *Early Childhood Indicators of Progress: Minnesota's Early Learning Standards* (2005), which provides an overview of developmental milestones for preschoolers. The understanding behind the standards is that children are on a continuum developmentally. The language of the standards, describing children's skills and behaviors can seem abstract and technical, so I have added some examples to illustrate how these apply to what children are doing in real life. To provide more context as you read, think of a child you know well and imagine his or her actions.

Social and Emotional Development

Early Childhood Indicators of Progress*

Children show progress in **emotional development** when they:

1. Demonstrate increasing competency in recognizing and describing own emotions

2. Demonstrate increasing use of words instead of actions to express emotions

3. Begin to understand and respond to others' emotions

4. Begin to show self-regulation to handle emotions appropriately

5. Explore a wide range of emotions in different ways (e.g., through play, art, music, dance)

6. Respond to praise, limits, and correction

*These indicators apply to children in the preschool period of ages three to five. They are based on expectations for children approximately four years of age.

⌒⎯⎯⎯⎯ *Lisa has been working for ten minutes on a compli-cated puzzle. After several tries, she cannot complete it. She goes to the teacher, puts her hands on her hips, and says with a scowl, "Ms. Barbara, I am really, really, really frustrated! I can't do it. Help me, please!"*

Early Childhood Indicators of Progress*

Children show progress in **self-concept** when they:

1. Begin to experiment with own potential and show confidence in own abilities

2. Demonstrate increasing self-direction and independence

3. Develop an awareness of self as having certain abilities, charac-teristics, and preferences

4. Begin to develop awareness, knowledge, and acceptance of own gender and cultural identity

⌒⎯⎯⎯⎯ *Joey is on the jungle gym. He crosses over the narrow bridge. He advances slowly and carefully, one step at a time, balanc-ing himself with his arms. When he gets to the other side, he smiles proudly, throws up his arms, and shouts "Look, I did it!"*

Early Childhood Indicators of Progress*

Children show progress in **social competence and relationships** when they:

1. Interact easily with one or more children

2. Interact easily with familiar adults

3. Approach others with expectations of positive interactions

4. Begin to participate successfully as a member of a group

---

*These indicators apply to children in the preschool period of ages three to five. They are based on expectations for children approximately four years of age.

5. Use play to explore, practice, and understand social roles and relationships

6. Begin to understand others' rights and privileges

7. Sustain interaction by cooperating, helping, sharing, and expressing interest

8. Seek adult help when needed for emotional support, physical assistance, social interaction, and approval

9. Use words and other constructive strategies to resolve conflicts

> *Paula observes quietly as two children—a girl and a boy—make vegetable soup in the housekeeping area. After a few minutes, Paula approaches them and asks, "Can I play?" The children ignore her. She stands, smiles, gets a little closer, and says softly but assertively, "I make chicken soup." The boy notices, looks at her, and responds, "Okay." Paula joins the little group, and they all continue to play together.*

Approaches to Learning

*Early Childhood Indicators of Progress**

Children show progress in **curiosity** when they:

1. Show eagerness and a sense of wonder as a learner

2. Show interest in discovering and learning new things

*Early Childhood Indicators of Progress**

Children show progress in **risk-taking** when they:

1. Choose new as well as a variety of familiar activities

2. Use a variety of strategies to solve problems

---

*These indicators apply to children in the preschool period of ages three to five. They are based on expectations for children approximately four years of age.

Early Childhood Indicators of Progress*

Children show progress in **imagination and invention** when they:

1. Approach tasks and experiences with flexibility, imagination, and inventiveness

2. Use new ways or novel strategies to solve problems or explore objects

3. Try out various pretend roles in play or with make-believe objects

⌒───◡   *Daniela's first language is Spanish, and Poua's first language is Hmong, and they both are learning English. They are playing in the beauty shop, pretending to put on nail polish, when Daniela says, "Red." However, the small bottle they are using is white. Poua looks around knowingly, goes to the art shelf, brings back a red marker, and hands it to Daniela, saying, "Red." They scribble on the bottle until it is red, giggling. Then they happily apply the imaginary "red" nail polish they have created together.*

Early Childhood Indicators of Progress*

Children show progress in **persistence** when they:

1. Work at a task despite distractions or interruptions

2. Seek and/or accept help or information when needed

3. Demonstrate ability to complete a task or stay engaged in an experience

---

*These indicators apply to children in the preschool period of ages three to five. They are based on expectations for children approximately four years of age.

Early Childhood Indicators of Progress*

Children show progress in **reflection and interpretation** when they:

1. Think about events and experiences and apply this knowledge to new situations

2. Generate ideas, suggestions, and/or make predictions

Language and Literacy Development

Early Childhood Indicators of Progress*

Children show progress in **listening** when they:

1. Understand nonverbal and verbal cues

2. Listen with understanding to stories, directions, and conversations

3. Follow directions that involve a two- or three-step sequence of actions

4. Listen to and recognize different sounds in rhymes and familiar words

Early Childhood Indicators of Progress*

Children show progress in **speaking** when they:

1. Communicate needs, wants, or thoughts through nonverbal gestures, actions, expressions, and/or words

2. Communicate information using home language and/or English

3. Speak clearly enough to be understood in home language and/or English

4. Use language for a variety of purposes

---

*These indicators apply to children in the preschool period of ages three to five. They are based on expectations for children approximately four years of age.

5. Use increasingly complex and varied vocabulary and language

6. Initiate, ask questions, and respond in conversation with others

> *During free playtime, Raoul and Matteo are making plans for a weekend visit to Matteo's house. They discuss what toys Raoul should bring to "play mechanics in the auto shop." Then the teacher calls the boys for story time and reads a book about polar bears, a completely different topic from their previous conversation. They listen attentively, make comments, and ask questions about polar bears.*

Early Childhood Indicators of Progress*

Children show progress in **emergent reading** when they:

1. Initiate stories and respond to stories told or read aloud

2. Represent stories told or read aloud through various media or during play

3. Guess what will happen next in a story using pictures as a guide

4. Retell information from a story

5. Show beginning understanding of concepts about print

6. Recognize and name some letters of the alphabet, especially those in own name

7. Begin to associate sounds with words or letters

> *During circle time, Sally sits in the teacher's chair and begins to "read" a book to three other children, who listen to her intently. She points to the pictures and follows the text with a plastic pointer, describing each page from memory. When Sally reaches the end of the story, she proclaims, "The end!"*

---

*These indicators apply to children in the preschool period of ages three to five. They are based on expectations for children approximately four years of age.

Early Childhood Indicators of Progress*

Children show progress in **emergent writing** when they:

1. Understand that writing is a way of communicating

2. Use scribbles, shapes, pictures, or dictation to represent thoughts or ideas

3. Engage in writing using letter-like symbols to make letters or words

4. Begin to copy or write own name

Rosa and Maia are in the dramatic play area, which is set up as a pizza parlor. One is a cook and the other is a waitress. They call out to Maggie, the classroom aide, "Do you want to order pizza?" As soon as Maggie sits down, Maia hands her the menu and explains the different types of pizza, pointing at the pictures. She scribbles the order on her notepad and takes it to Rosa, who studies it carefully and asks, "Is this order for one or two people? I only see one here." When Maia confirms the order is for two customers, Rosa adds her own note on the paper and goes to the kitchen to prepare the pizzas.

Creativity and the Arts

Early Childhood Indicators of Progress*

Children show progress in **creating** when they:

1. Use a variety of media and materials for exploration and creative expression

2. Participate in art and music experiences

3. Participate in creative movement, drama, and dance

---

*These indicators apply to children in the preschool period of ages three to five. They are based on expectations for children approximately four years of age.

Early Childhood Indicators of Progress*

Children show progress in **responding** when they:

1. Show others and/or talk about what they have made or done

2. Show interest and respect for the creative work of self and others

Early Childhood Indicators of Progress*

Children show progress in **evaluating** when they:

1. Share experiences, ideas, and thoughts about art and creative expression

2. Share opinions about likes and dislikes in art and creative expression

> *Marysol has been painting at the easel for ten minutes. In this classroom, children have been studying nature in the spring, including landscape illustrations. The teacher says, "Marysol, tell me about your painting." Marysol responds, "This is the yellow sun and a tree and flowers, and the sun makes the flowers grow."*

Cognitive Development

Early Childhood Indicators of Progress*

Children show progress in **mathematical and logical thinking** when they:

NUMBER CONCEPTS AND OPERATIONS

1. Demonstrate increasing interest in and awareness of numbers and counting

2. Demonstrate understanding of one-to-one correspondence between objects and number

---

*These indicators apply to children in the preschool period of ages three to five. They are based on expectations for children approximately four years of age.

3. Demonstrate ability to count in sequence

4. Demonstrate ability to state the number that comes next up to 9 or 10

5. Demonstrate beginning ability to combine and separate numbers of objects

PATTERNS AND RELATIONSHIPS

6. Recognize and duplicate simple patterns

7. Sort objects into subgroups by one or two characteristics

8. Order or sequence several objects on the basis of one characteristic

SPATIAL RELATIONSHIPS/GEOMETRY

9. Identify and name common shapes

10. Use words that show understanding of order and position of objects

MEASUREMENT

11. Recognize objects can be measured by height, length, weight, and time

12. Make comparisons between at least two groups of objects

MATHEMATICAL REASONING

13. Use simple strategies to solve mathematical problems

⌒   *Pao and Arthur are standing at the whiteboard. Pao is counting aloud, "One, two, three, five." Arthur scribbles symbols with a marker to represent numbers. Suddenly, they realize their counting is not sequential. They go back to the manipulatives table and practice counting small teddy bears very slowly: "One, two, three, four, five—we forgot four. We forgot four!" The children laugh,*

---

*These indicators apply to children in the preschool period of ages three to five. They are based on expectations for children approximately four years of age.

satisfied with their discovery, and go back to the whiteboard to write the number four between the three and the five.

Early Childhood Indicators of Progress*

Children show progress in **scientific thinking and problem-solving** when they:

OBSERVING

1. Use senses to explore materials and the environment

2. Identify and/or describe objects by physical characteristics

QUESTIONING

3. Express wonder about the natural world

4. Ask questions and seek answers through active exploration

5. Make predictions about objects and natural events

INVESTIGATING

6. Use tools (e.g., magnifying glass, binoculars, maps) for investigation of the environment

7. Make comparisons between objects that have been collected or observed

Jill is at the water table, where the teacher has set up floating and sinking objects. Jill tries to sink the small red boat with her hands, but it keeps floating back up when she lets go. After a few tries, she decides to put a big stone on the boat. The boat goes to the bottom. Jill looks surprised, then lifts the stone and watches the boat come back up. She keeps experimenting with different-sized stones. When another child joins her, Jill comments, "The big stone makes the boat sink. It can float with the little stone."

---

*These indicators apply to children in the preschool period of ages three to five. They are based on expectations for children approximately four years of age.

Early Childhood Indicators of Progress*

Children show progress in **social systems understanding** when they:

HUMAN RELATIONSHIPS

1. Recognize and appreciate similarities and differences between self and others from diverse backgrounds

2. Understand various family roles, jobs, rules, and relationships

3. Participate in activities to help others in the community

UNDERSTANDING THE WORLD

4. Recognize and describe the roles of workers in the community

5. Share responsibility in taking care of their environment

6. Begin to recall recent and past events

7. Identify characteristics of the places where they live and play within their community

8. Begin to understand the uses of media and technology and how they affect their lives

Luisito is Latino. Mohamed and Ali are Somali. They all live in a rural community in the Midwest. At lunchtime, Mohamed and Ali announce that they want to speak Spanish like Luisito. They make up words to end with "-to" and "-ta." All three giggle as they continue to experiment with the sounds of Spanish. When the teacher points out that people speak different languages in different parts of the world, Luisito confirms, "My grandma speaks Spanish in Mexico."

*These indicators apply to children in the preschool period of ages three to five. They are based on expectations for children approximately four years of age.

Physical and Motor Development

*Early Childhood Indicators of Progress**

Children show progress in **gross motor development** when they:

1. Develop large muscle control and coordination

2. Develop body strength, balance, flexibility, and stamina

3. Use a variety of equipment for physical development

4. Develop ability to move their body in space with coordination

*Early Childhood Indicators of Progress**

Children show progress in **fine motor development** when they:

1. Develop small muscle control and coordination

2. Use eye-hand coordination to perform a variety of tasks

3. Explore and experiment with a variety of tools (e.g., spoons, crayons, paintbrushes, scissors, keyboards)

*Early Childhood Indicators of Progress**

Children show progress in **physical health and well-being** when they:

1. Participate in a variety of physical activities to enhance personal health and physical fitness

2. Follow basic health and safety rules

3. Recognize and eat a variety of nutritious foods

4. Demonstrate increasing independence with basic self-care skills

Under the cool arcade of a California preschool, Tomi is riding a tricycle, controlling the speed with his strong little legs and expertly avoiding obstacles. He stops at the play farmers' market set

---

*These indicators apply to children in the preschool period of ages three to five. They are based on expectations for children approximately four years of age.

up by his teacher. He buys zucchini and red peppers, because, he says, "Vegetables are good. They help you grow strong." Then he pays for the vegetables by writing his name on a check.

The Role of Language and Literacy in School Readiness

The 1998 National Research Council report *Preventing Reading Difficulties in Young Children* has helped shape the definition of school readiness (Snow, Burns, and Griffin 1998). The report focuses on the importance of language and early literacy in learning to read. It makes it clear that the foundation for academic skills is the ability to talk, read, and write. For example, in order to write a story about butterflies, the child has to ask questions about butterflies (talk), do research in books or on the Internet (read), and put ideas on paper or on the computer (write).

The best tool for getting along with others and managing our own behavior is language. Sara, who is four years old, says (talk) she wants to play with the truck that Peter is holding. She notices he is not letting it go on his own. She has to make a choice: she can grab the truck from Peter (not talk), play with something else (not talk), or say, "Peter, I want a turn with the truck" (talk). When we tell children to use their words, it is always as the alternative to the more primitive behaviors of hitting, grabbing, or whining. Without effective language and communication skills, it is impossible to achieve good social-emotional development. That is why there is a special emphasis on language as the key to school readiness.

Analysis of Omar's School Readiness

Think about Omar again and his first day of kindergarten. Using the *Early Childhood Indicators of Progress: Minnesota's Early Learning Standards* (2005), I have prepared a summary to help analyze his school readiness, including concrete examples to assess his experiences and to imagine how his school readiness would look in very practical terms.

Early Learning Standard	Summary of Critical Early Childhood Indicators of Progress	What We See Omar Doing
Social and Emotional Development	Interacts easily with other children and adults Uses words to resolve conflicts Participates successfully as a group member	Smiles Responds to teacher Greets classmates by waving Sits in circle
Approaches to Learning	Is curious Takes risks Approaches tasks with flexibility, imagination, and inventiveness Is persistent and reflective	Chooses a marker in his favorite color to show how he writes his name
Language and Literacy Development	Uses language to communicate needs Interacts socially with others Shares ideas, thoughts, and feelings Builds on spoken and written language abilities	Responds nonverbally to the principal Speaks to the teacher in telegraphic English Says good morning in his home language, Spanish Writes his name Remembers the story
Creativity and the Arts	Uses various media and materials for exploration and creative expression Creates Responds Evaluates	Shows a marked preference for the color blue Chooses the marker he likes best
Cognitive Development	Acquires information Thinks logically Orders and puts in sequence Understands measurement Engages in scientific thinking and problem solving Understands social systems	Understands counting as a concept Knows that not all his classmates speak Spanish
Physical and Motor Development	Develops large-muscle control Hones small-muscle control Is in good physical health	Uses small muscles to hold the marker and write his name Forms letters correctly Passes the preschool health screening Has all the required immunizations

Even though this is only Omar's first day of kindergarten and we haven't yet observed all his abilities, we can start to picture where he is on the road to being ready for school. Many of his behaviors are due to his maturity as a five-year-old. Some behaviors are because of work his preschool teachers and family have done up to this point. And other behaviors can be credited to positive connections that his elementary school's staff made with him and his family.

In addition to his own developmental path, Omar has had many opportunities for learning. The results of this are the developmentally appropriate social and academic skills he demonstrates. Socially, he seems comfortable with new adults like the principal and teacher, he can follow directions, and he functions well in a group of peers. Academically, he can write his name, he knows how to count to ten, and he understands the story.

Omar has the skills to enter kindergarten. As a child of an immigrant family, he is part of a group of children who statistically are not doing well in school. How the preschool program and his mother have prepared him is only one side of the story. In order to succeed in the rest of his educational career, he needs the strong support of his elementary school.

Demographics and the Learning Needs of Children in the Twenty-first Century

The first recommendation of the 2009 National Association for the Education of Young Children (NAEYC) Position Statement on Developmentally Appropriate Practice is to create a caring community of learners by being sensitive to the individual development and learning needs of all children. The U.S. Census Bureau estimates that in 2000, approximately 20 percent of children lived in immigrant families. More than 40 percent of Latino children and more than 30 percent of Asian American children lived in families with a father or mother who did not speak English fluently. By the year 2030, the projections are that 51 percent of children in the United States will be children of color—African American, Asian American, or Latino—compared to 25 percent in 1990. Based on a basic budget-poverty measure, which includes the cost of health insurance and child care, approximately 50 to 60 percent of young children who are Latino, African American, American Indian, or Native Hawaiian or other Pacific Islander are poor compared with approximately 30 percent of white and Asian children (Hernandez, Denton, and Macartney 2007).

School data and research show that many poor children, children of color, and children of immigrants do not do well in school. They are not ready for school before they enter, and once there they have increasing difficulties academically and socially (Brooks-Gunn 2008). They are not proficient at grade level in math and reading, and they are more likely to be suspended for inappropriate behavior. African American and Latino children have the lowest scores in academic and behavior assessments (Brooks-Gunn, Rouse, and McLanahan 2007).

Kindergarten teachers describe these children as having more difficulties in adjusting to school. Sadly, this gap appears to grow as children move into elementary school and high school, and they drop out of school at alarming rates. These statistics call for an intentional planning effort to ensure all children are well taught in a system that is struggling to meet their needs. Not only do educators need to pay attention to the developmental needs of children, but they also have to be competent at addressing, valuing, and using cultural and linguistic differences to teach (Villegas and Lucas 2002; Copple 2003).

The Concept of Ready Schools

Last winter, Ms. Annie, Omar's kindergarten teacher, attended a joint-staff workshop with the principal of the school where she teaches and with Head Start staff. The idea originated at a school district principals' meeting earlier in the fall. The workshop topic and agenda were straightforward—share expectations and classroom routines. After a general introduction and information about the demographics of their community, teachers, paraprofessionals, and administrators divided into small groups to discuss what they teach as well as *how* they teach in their programs and classrooms. They also talked about how they work with families.

The education professionals reviewed a checklist as a guide to define the activities that helped children and families transition from pre-K to kindergarten. At the end of three hours, the evaluations showed that participants felt productive and were grateful to know each other's approach better. A recommendation was made to have a similar workshop every year and to invite more preschool programs from the area.

In 1990, President George H. W. Bush created the National Education Goals Panel to review the quality of education in the United States. Goal 1: Ready to Learn stated that by the year 2000 all children in America would start school ready to learn. The goal was ambitious and is still a work in progress as educators, researchers, and policy makers continue to find solutions. In pursuit of this goal, experts discussed the role of schools in welcoming children, and from this the concept of ready schools emerged.

In 1998, the panel convened a special group of advisors who suggested the Ten Keys to Ready Schools in their report *Ready Schools* (Shore 1998, 5). The Ready Schools Resource Group based its recommendations on a review of research and best practices. Today these recommendations are still very relevant and include the following:

1. Ready schools smooth the transition between home and school.

2. Ready schools strive for continuity between early care and education programs and elementary schools.

3. Ready schools help children learn and make sense of their complex and exciting world.

4. Ready schools are committed to the success of every child.

5. Ready schools are committed to the success of every teacher and every adult who interacts with children during the school day.

6. Ready schools introduce or expand approaches that have been shown to raise achievement.

7. Ready schools are learning organizations that alter practices and programs if they do not benefit children.

8. Ready schools serve children in communities.

9. Ready schools take responsibility for results.

10. Ready schools have strong leadership.

So, is Omar's school ready for him? Using this list, let's see in what ways Omar's new school is ready for children:

- The principals in the school district made a plan to address continuity in their community between the preschool and the elementary worlds. The principals convened staff from preschools and elementary schools to meet each other and share their work so they could be more successful (#2, #5, #8, and # 10).

- Ms. Annie and the principal participated in joint training with the Head Start staff to coordinate the curriculum (#2).

- The school organized a picnic before the first day so children and their families could meet the staff and visit the school (#1 and #4).

- Ms. Annie did the sign-in activity and read a book, following the preschool routine in the Head Start classroom (#1).
- Ms. Annie acknowledged and welcomed the cultural and linguistic diversity in her classroom (#3).

With the information from this first day, we can see that eight of the ten items have been addressed. Omar's school is intentional in getting ready for children and their families, which is not a simple task.

Ready Schools Need Ready Personnel

Schools are more than buildings. Schools are places where teachers, educational assistants, nurses, custodians, social workers, cooks, secretaries, bus drivers, and principals work directly with children and families. These staff members are important in the students' lives. They interact with children every day in classrooms, in hallways, in lunchrooms, and on the bus. Staff members have the power to send discouraging messages or to provide encouraging support. To be ready for the children who are entering kindergarten and their families, school personnel have to prepare themselves. There is a lot they think about: Who are the children coming to our school? What do they need? Where were they before coming to us? How will our teaching methods work for them? Who are their families? What are their expectations? What do we expect from children and families? How do we communicate effectively with them? The most important question, one not always asked explicitly, is do we think these children can really learn and succeed?

In a study conducted by the National Center for Education Statistics (1993), only about a third of kindergarten teachers believed that children would be ready to advance to first grade. Other research tells us that teachers tend to rate children of color lower in social competence (Doucet and Tudge 2007). This happens when children respond inappropriately to the communication style of the school culture. For example, children may be used to a direct style at home, such as "Ramon, put away your toys now." But often teachers use an indirect style, by asking questions, such as "Ramon, would you like to put away the toys?" If Ramon wants to continue to play and truthfully answers, "No," he will likely be labeled as defiant.

In diverse countries such as the United States, demographic patterns are not static. Children, families, and staff from many cultures mix and interact in schools. This creates challenges for educational systems that are mandated to teach *all* children.

Education Is a Complex Professional Field

Every other summer, I teach a two-day special topics course at the University of Minnesota. The students are practicing teachers who use continuing education credits for their licensure. One hot day, when the air-conditioning was struggling to keep up, our class had a lively discussion on the status of teachers in society. When I pointed out that teachers are part of the intellectual elite, a young man wearing shorts and sandals looked at his feet and said defiantly, "I don't see any wing tips, do you?" One could argue that the young man felt comfortable wearing such casual clothes at a university because he is indeed part of the elite. Clothes do not matter as much when someone is smart and part of the "culture of power." Being part of the culture of power means knowing the rules that define talking, writing, and interacting—all of which are important to getting things done and being part of the inner circle (Delpit 1995). This is in contrast to how many families feel, whether they are immigrant or American born, particularly the families who have low educational levels.

In order to be licensed to teach, all kindergarten teachers in elementary school need to have a college degree. That puts them in a category of nearly one-third of the total adult population who are at the highest level of education (U.S. Census 2005). At the same time, about one-quarter of parents have a college degree (Hernandez, Denton, and Macartney 2007). To borrow a phrase from *Other People's Children: Cultural Conflict in the Classroom* (Delpit 1995), many teachers are teaching other people's children. This idea refers not only to racial and cultural differences but also to being distanced from children by education and social class. I believe it is important to be aware of the issue so it can be addressed directly and appropriately in preservice training and in continuing professional development (Passe 1994; Villegas and Lucas 2002). Schools can then be fully ready to welcome all children and families.

The fact is that the field of education for noneducators is as complex as any other professional field, including medicine or law. School Web sites, brochures, and staff use jargon such as *interdisciplinary, curriculum objectives, math recovery,* and *robotics electives.* Parents want to know what these words mean and how they will help children learn.

Families' Hopes and Anxieties

When children enter kindergarten, their families want to become more familiar with the culture of education. They want to know what the rules are so they can help their children achieve, because all families want their children to do well in school. When I conduct workshops and focus groups, I see that parents, regardless of background, have similar anxieties. Families look to educators to serve as their guides through the culture of education:

- "We cannot judge the quality of education. We are not experts, and we just hope that the school provides quality education." (a Laotian father)

- "I want to help my son be a better student, but I don't know how. You need to tell us how to do that." (a Hmong mother)

- "We want our children to be ready for college, like the district says, but we don't know how to get from kindergarten to college." (a Latino father)

- "I don't want the teacher to love my child—I already love her. I want the teacher to *teach* my daughter what she needs to learn." (a teen mother)

Family-School Partnerships Are a Special Effort

The barriers for developing good family-school partnerships fall into one of two categories: structure or attitude (Christenson 1999). On the structural side, the school staff may not have had training in how to work with parents. Also, schools may not provide an activities schedule that is convenient for parents (Pianta and Kraft-Sayre 2003). As a result, the opportunities to partner are few. The communication system that tells families what is happening at school may be written and formal, using newsletters and flyers, whereas parents might use an informal, word-of-mouth system in person and on the phone. In one focus group, a Somali father said that his community is so well-connected by cell phone that if his son's school wanted to let him know of an important event they could call his cousin in Kenya and within minutes he would hear about it in Minnesota!

On the attitude side, the staff may not be interested in considering the points of view and needs of families. Teachers want to have partnerships with families, but often on their own terms (Bowman 1999). The economic, educational, and social distance between families and teachers causes misunderstandings. For example, I once heard kindergarten teachers lament that Latino families send their little girls dressed up in frilly dresses and patent leather shoes on the first day of school. They commented that these parents just don't value education, don't understand that in kindergarten children do messy activities, which is how they learn. These teachers needed to hear the reasons why Latino girls come dressed up on the first day of school. They needed to know that the parents wanted to present their little girls in the best light to make a good impression on the teacher. The children were dressed up and had their hair combed in fancy ways to look beautiful and attractive. The parents also assume that at the "big" school their children sit neatly at their desks to learn. These parents show they value education when they send their children to school well-kempt and well-behaved—these are the qualities they believe make children ready for school. The problem is not that the parents don't value education, but that they don't know how young children learn and how kindergarten teachers teach. They don't have the inside information.

Educators as Cultural Guides

A big part of Omar's positive experience with the transition to kindergarten was the guidance his mother, Olga, received. While Omar was in the preschool program at Head Start, Olga was personally invited to monthly events from January to April. Each month's topic was offered on a schedule that included morning, afternoon, and evening options. These options made it convenient for her to attend the workshops, since her shift as a grocery-store cashier changed every ten days.

In addition to information on child development, Olga learned about how to choose a school and tips to help children transition to kindergarten. She liked best the session where a kindergarten teacher and a principal came to talk about how schools work. Olga learned about the differences between Head Start and elementary school and about the expectations for parent involvement. She understood that in the school, parents have to take more initiative in connecting with staff than they did in Head Start. In general, schools do not have as many family liaisons to help parents. The highlight was a PowerPoint slide showing the road from kindergarten to college, as well as the advice of the principal, who said, "If you do all the things we have talked about, your child will have the best chance of going to college."

Throughout the winter, spring, and summer, Olga received valuable tips and new ideas to help her understand the culture of education. Both the preschool and elementary staff acted as cultural guides to an aspect of life in which she had little experience. They did so in a direct way, knowing she had high aspirations for her child's education but little knowledge about how to navigate the educational system.

Omar's mom felt encouraged and motivated to attend the orientation at the school, play with Omar on the school playground during the summer, help Omar write his name at home, and take him to storytime at the library. All of these activities made sense to her in the context of helping Omar with his education over the long term.

Discussion Starters

- Look at the *Early Childhood Indicators of Progress: Minnesota's Early Learning Standards* list in this chapter (pages 16–28). Make a mark by all the items that depend on language skills to fully develop. How are language and literacy, cognitive development, and social-emotional development interrelated?

- Pretend that you are taking a trip to the Grand Canyon and you are hiring a guide. What do you want from this guide? What do you want the guide to say and do? What characteristics do you expect the guide to have? Make a list. How would the items you listed apply to educators helping parents learn about the educational system?

- Find and read the early learning standards for your state at the National Child Care Information and Technical Assistance Center Web site at http://nccic.acf.hhs.gov. Discuss how your knowledge of the early learning standards guides the way you work with children. If this is your first experience with such standards, discuss how they will guide your work in the future. Choose three indicators you want to focus on.

CHAPTER 2

Kindergarten in the Twenty-first Century

At a Minnesota Kindergarten Association conference, I am presenting a transition-to-kindergarten workshop to early childhood educators and kindergarten teachers. A show of hands reveals that the participants are between twenty-five and sixty years old, and the majority have more than ten years of working experience. As a warm-up activity, I ask participants to share their kindergarten memories with the person sitting next to them. After a moment of silent reflection, a crescendo of voices fills the room. Faces are animated—some smiling, others frowning. There is laughter and empathetic listening. Everyone is engaged, and I hate to break up the conversation, but we need to move on.

To the larger group, participants present the main points of their exchanges. First, they still remembered kindergarten! For many it was a sweet time of playing, making friends, and sharing snacks in the care of a friendly teacher. For a few, kindergarten was a painful time, saying good-bye to their mom or siblings, or not having a nice teacher. Only two people in the group did not go to kindergarten at all; their families kept them at home until first grade.

A Brief History of Kindergarten

Friedrich Froebel, a German educator, opened the first kindergarten in Blankenburg, Germany, in 1837. During the 1830s and 1840s he developed his vision for kindergarten based on the ideas of the French philosopher Jean-Jacques Rousseau and the later Swiss educator Johann Heinrich Pestalozzi. These progressive education reformers introduced the concept that children were naturally good and active learners. At the time, this thinking was quite radical. The common belief until then had been that children were little creatures who needed stern handling to become good adults. Play was seen as a waste of time and proof that children should be tamed so they could be more productive.

Undaunted, Froebel argued that teachers should use music, nature study, stories, and dramatic play to teach children. He encouraged the use of crafts and manipulatives, such as small building blocks or puzzles. He also promoted the idea of circle time for children to learn in a group. Froebel proposed that children acquire cognitive and social skills by using their natural curiosity and desire to learn. He believed women had the best sensitivity and qualities to work with young children in developing their emotional skills. Consequently, Froebel opened a training school just for women.

Froebel's ideas were so new that the Prussian government closed all kindergartens in 1851, fearing a socialist revolutionary movement. Nevertheless, the concept spread quickly throughout the rest of the world, and by the end of the nineteenth century, many countries had started kindergartens for middle-class children. Then, between 1900 and the start of World War I, England and France began to establish free kindergartens for poor children. Kindergartens also reopened in Germany at the end of the nineteenth century, and they still serve children who are three to six years old. The word *kindergarten* means "garden of children," a beautiful metaphor for what happens there—children growing like flowers and plants, nurtured by a positive environment with good soil, rain, and sun, as well as an attentive gardener.

In the United States, Margarethe Schurz opened the first kindergarten in Watertown, Wisconsin, in 1856 for her immigrant German community. This kindergarten caught the attention of Elizabeth Peabody, who started the first American English-language kindergarten in Boston in 1860. Then, in large cities, charities began to fund private kindergartens to care for the three- to six-year-old children of immigrant factory workers, which meant these children were healthy, clean, fed, and clothed. The goal was not so much to teach reading and writing but to develop overall cognitive and social-emotional skills—the beginning of considering the *whole child*.

In 1873, Saint Louis, Missouri, became the first school district to have a public kindergarten. By 1914, the beginning of World War I, all the major American urban school systems had publicly funded kindergartens that were open for five-year-olds. Mississippi was the last state to offer public kindergarten, in 1986. Today, kindergarten is available in all states. Forty-two states mandate every school district to offer it. Children are eligible to attend kindergarten at the age of five, although some states allow for four-year-olds. In many states, the compulsory age for starting school ranges between six and eight years old, so families can decide to skip kindergarten and enter school in the first or second grade. In 2008, about four million children attended half-day or full-day kindergarten in the United States (Hussar and Bailey 2009).

Philosophical Foundation for the American Kindergarten

Many educators and psychologists have influenced the philosophy of the modern American kindergarten, including John Dewey, Maria Montessori, Erik Erikson, Jean Piaget, and Lev Vygotsky. To combine their ideas and create the ideal prekindergarten and kindergarten program, this is what the composite list would look like:

Theorist	Teaching and Learning Practices
Dewey (1859–1952)	• Teachers share their knowledge with children • Children learn from building on their knowledge of the world by adding new information and active exploration
Montessori (1870–1952)	• Teachers provide child-centered environments, with materials, books, and toys that are accessible, orderly, and beautiful • Children learn by structuring their own time, being responsible for their environment, and using repetition
Erikson (1902–1994)	• Teachers set clear expectations, encourage children to be independent, and give feedback on learning • Children develop purpose and competence by using real tools and solving real problems
Piaget (1896–1980)	• Teachers provide open-ended activities and questions to help children learn to think • Children move their thinking from perception to reasoning
Vygotsky (1896–1934)	• Teachers provide positive challenges and support (scaffolding) to stretch learning • Children learn through interaction, experimentation, and conversation

Common Points of Quality for Pre-K and Kindergarten

• Strong and meaningful curriculum, relevant to children
• Purposeful activity
• Learning can be uncomfortable
• Learning becomes fun when children are engaged and supported
• Balance of child-initiated and teacher-led activities
• Real life exploration and problem solving
• Free play is not free; it is active learning during an extended period of time where children choose among equally valuable activities
• Children are challenged in a positive way
• Play is a child's work
• Language is essential to learn
• Interactions with adults and peers are important for learning
• Learning and growing does not happen naturally; it needs to be planned and nurtured

Table content drawn from Mooney, Carol Garhart. 2000. *Theories of childhood: An introduction to Dewey, Montessori, Erikson, Piaget, and Vygotsky.* St. Paul: Redleaf Press.

The Reality of the Current Kindergarten

You may be wondering why the transition from preschool to kindergarten is a big deal if both preschool and kindergarten fall under the category of early childhood education (Copple and Bredekamp 2009). By definition, shouldn't they already be aligned? This is not always the case. The legacy of Dewey, Montessori, Erikson, Piaget, and Vygotsky is visible in many kindergartens, although there are some misinterpretations along the way (Mooney 2000).

Some classrooms are perfect examples of the previous table's right column, Common Points of Quality for Pre-K and Kindergarten. However, in an extensive study conducted in early childhood, kindergarten, and first-grade classrooms, only about 14 percent scored high in measures of classroom organization, emotional support, and instructional support (Hamre and Pianta 2007). Across the United States, the quality of classrooms is vastly variable. Some classrooms have a strong thematic curriculum with well-integrated activities and a sensitive, intentional teacher. This is the best situation, one in which children should learn. Other classrooms have a curriculum that is an eclectic collection of unrelated activities presented by a warm and friendly teacher. The children may not be learning much, but the emphasis is on fun. Still other classrooms have a curriculum that is not relevant to the children and is presented by a teacher who is unaware of children's learning needs or inattentive to them. This lack of consistency does not serve children well.

New Academic Pressures

As the door to the "serious learning years," kindergarten is under pressure. Should we keep the more relaxed pace of pre-K, or should we "push down" the first-grade curriculum, applying it to kindergarten in an effort to speed up learning? Some people worry that we may be pressuring children too much, while other people are near panic wondering if children will ever catch up if they are not yet ready for kindergarten.

As the movement for accountability in education grows, forty-two states have aligned learning expectations for kindergarten with elementary and secondary standards (Olson 2007). At first glance, learning standards in kindergarten do not appear to be that different from the early learning standards listed in chapter 1.

Nostalgically, adults may perceive kindergarten as the basis for formal education. Most people remember it as a time to make friends and learn the rules of school before the "real work" begins. Kindergarten teachers now are feeling increasing pressure to prepare children for first grade, with prescribed math and reading curricula and an intense schedule of assessments. Kindergarten is the bridge between early education and elementary education; it is not a practice grade anymore. It is serious business.

Full-Day versus Half-Day Kindergarten

Kindergarten was conceived as a half-day program, based on the idea that a full day of school was too long for young children. A half day was supposed to ensure a low-key introduction to school, with longer days starting in first grade. The argument that children cannot handle full-time schedules outside of their home is not as relevant anymore. As families' work patterns have changed, more children are now in full-day child care. Approximately 80 percent of all kindergartners have had one year of preschool, and 50 percent of kindergartners have had two years of preschool (Barnett et al. 2008). More children are accustomed to a full-day schedule. All-day kindergarten may even be easier on children, since it eliminates an extra transition to child care.

Kindergarten as the Bridge between Preschool and Elementary School

Children's experiences vary greatly before they enter kindergarten. They may be at home with mom or dad or at grandma's house. They may be in a large child care center or in a small family child care home. They may attend Head Start or a public school readiness program. Or they may be in a combination of places, depending on their families' income, mobility, and needs for child care.

Preschool quality is undependable as a decentralized system (Pianta et al. 1999). Some centers and homes have teachers and providers who are caring and sensitive. They scaffold children's learning with meaningful activities and language, using a research-based curriculum in a literacy-rich environment. They assess children's learning with developmentally appropriate tools. In other settings, children may spend hours on end watching TV in a barren environment with a caregiver who does not speak or read to them (NACCRRA 2008).

The Impact of Home on School Preparation

Children's home lives prepare them for school in different ways too (Hart and Risley 1995). Some children have literacy- and language-rich homes with many books. They have parents and relatives who talk, read, and write with them in ways similar to how learning happens at school. These children learn the basics of conversation, critical thinking, and making choices from the time they are babies. They receive encouragement for being learners and thinkers. Their parents tend to have a high level of education and are literate in English and in their home language. In these families, children usually practice school-like activities such as reading, drawing, scribbling, and playing board games or language-based what-if games. The following interaction between a dad and his preschool son illustrates the point:

Son: What are we doing, Daddy?

Father: We are waiting for the elevator. It will take us to the third floor. That's where we parked the car.

Son: Where are we now?

Father: We are on the first floor. Do you see the numbers next to the door? One, two, three, four, five. We are going to three. It's here. Let's get in.

Father: (in the elevator) Do you see the numbers again? Can you push the "three" button?

Son: (squealing in delight) I did it, Daddy! I pushed the three!

Father: Yeah! Three, like you. You are three too! You are actually three and a half—that's more than three.

Son: (following the numbers as the elevator ascends) Look, we are at three.

Father: Yes, we are here. Let's go quickly. . . .

We can safely say this child is getting ready for kindergarten. His father is teaching him numbers and having conversations in a natural way. Not every child has opportunities like this, and it becomes necessary for early educators to ensure such opportunities are provided in early childhood classrooms or child care homes.

Some families can even indoctrinate their children into literacy. On a flight from Phoenix to Minneapolis, I spent three-and-a-half hours seated next to a mother and her three-year-old daughter. As an unrepentant early childhood observer, I found the scene fascinating! The mother had prepared a full bag of learning artifacts—books, markers, rulers, alphabet templates, and small toys—to keep her little girl occupied and happy. During the trip, they played, talked, read, drew, and wrote. Literacy, learning, entertainment, and behavior management were all happening seamlessly. This little girl was also getting ready for kindergarten.

Many children may be well cared for in nurturing homes, but they may not be engaged in preliteracy activities in the normal course of their day. Here's an example of a Hmong father's concerns about his children. The father's grandparents care for his children while he and his wife work during the day. He said, "My grandparents are nice people. They are good about feeding the children and making sure they are safe, but the children watch TV all day. I am not sure that's good for them."

The risk factors for not being ready for school fall into four categories: the mother's education is less than high school; the family income is below the poverty line; the family is headed by a single parent; or the primary language is other than English and the adults are not literate in English or their home language. These risk factors are cumulative, with some children experiencing more than one (West, Denton, and Reaney 2000).

Some children arrive at the kindergarten door with the language and social skills necessary to learn, and others are behind. In many kindergarten classrooms, the level of language and literacy development may range from that of a three-year-old to that of an eight-year-old (Neuman, Copple, and Bredekamp 1999). As the bridge between the pre-K and the K-12 worlds, then, kindergarten has the tough job of being the *equalizer* grade to bring children up to speed.

What Kindergarten Looks Like Today

What would Friedrich Froebel think of the twenty-first century kindergarten? I think he would be happy to visit some modern kindergarten classrooms and see that circle time is still the preferred format for reading, singing, large-group demonstrations, and show-and-tell. Of course, circle time now happens on very colorful synthetic rugs with shapes, numbers, and alphabet letters, with furniture made of plastic in bright primary colors. In the housekeeping area, toy cell phones and cash registers make electronic beeps. In the refrigerator, the pretend food is multicultural and includes pizza, tacos, sushi, bagels, and eggplant. In the crib, the baby dolls are Caucasian, African American, and Asian. On the wall, posters display the alphabet, hand-washing instructions, and class rules that direct children to be respectful. Technology is now part of everyday learning with computers, listening centers, CD players, overhead projectors, and cameras.

Froebel would be impressed but maybe a little disoriented at first. The classroom might feel overstimulating. He might be surprised, but as a progressive thinker he would understand that a culture socializes its children for the world in which they need to function. Times have changed; the twenty-first century is fast paced, and its children need to learn to handle different sounds, visuals, and messages to be productive in the world outside of school.

He might be intrigued by the current emphasis on accountability. We assess children with preschool screening before they come to kindergarten or at the beginning of kindergarten. We test them again at the end of the year to see what they have learned. The issue of assessment is still somewhat confusing for early educators. The 2003 joint position statement of NAEYC and the National Association of Early Childhood Specialists in State Departments of Education calls assessment a *responsibility* of early educators and policy makers, which means that early educators need to understand how to assess children and know what to do with the information (McAfee, Leong, and Bodrova 2004).

Froebel might be concerned if he continued to visit schools and noticed that some kindergarten classrooms do not have toys, dramatic play areas, or blocks. Children sit in circle time but do much of their learning with worksheets. He might note that, after all these years, we do not have everything figured out!

Two Kindergarten Classrooms Observed

Like the teachers in *Miss Bindergarten Gets Ready for Kindergarten* (Slate and Wolff 1996), Ms. Gloria and Ms. Susan have spent the last week of August in staff development workshops. They have also prepared their classrooms for students by putting the blocks in their bins, the books on the shelf, and the plastic vegetables in the housekeeping area. The word walls are organized, and the cubbies are labeled.

On the first day of school, twenty children arrive in each classroom, all dressed up, wearing school uniforms and new sneakers. They carry huge backpacks on their shoulders. Some children come with their parents, who did not want their children to take the bus on the first day; others get off the bus a bit tentatively, with a name tag on their chest. The youngest children are four-and-a-half years old, admitted under the early-entrance policy, and the oldest are already six years old, having been held back a year because their parents did not think they were ready for kindergarten when they were five. Some of the children are just beginning to use full sentences, and a few are already reading on their own.

During the August workshops, the principal of the school where Ms. Gloria and Ms. Susan teach had a PowerPoint presentation on data from the previous year's tests. The school district research and evaluation department has been able to correlate student achievement across four assessments: beginning kindergarten, end of kindergarten, end of first grade, and the third grade state test. If children meet the benchmarks at each of the first three points, there is a strong probability they will be able to pass the third grade test in reading and math. The third grade test is high stakes, as it determines the ranking of the school on the state list. The principal asked teachers to test the children every month to monitor their progress.

The school district also provided training on language and literacy, with specific recommendations for instruction, such as repeated reading, playing phonological awareness games during transitions, holding conversations during small group and mealtimes, and engaging parents through simple weekly home activities.

In this magnet school, which attracts families from many parts of the city, the income and education levels of the families are varied, as are the home experiences of the children. Ms. Gloria and Ms. Susan wonder what the year will bring.

Let's see what happens in the two kindergarten classrooms.

Ms. Gloria

Ms. Gloria's classroom is ready, and the children have arrived. She has been teaching for ten years, and on most days she enjoys her job.

Ms. Gloria found the training interesting, but she feels it is an added imposition. Although she is upset about all the pressure, she begins the year by setting her testing schedule. Every first week of the month, a volunteer from the university comes to assess the children. Some students are making good progress, and others are not. Ms. Gloria does not see the point of assessment. She thinks she could have guessed, without the test results, who was doing well—the children whose parents read to them at home and who value education. She has little hope for the others. Ms. Gloria's teaching methods are the same for all children, and she does not see how she could change them. She does not send parents activities to do at home unless they ask for them at the fall conference.

In this classroom, Ms. Gloria does most of the talking. Children are expected to be silent and obedient, and they spend a lot of time doing worksheets with numbers and letters. The classroom contains puzzles and manipulative toys, but it includes no dramatic or sensory-play options. There is no thematic curriculum. Ms. Gloria says that with all these academics, there is no time left to play.

Ms. Susan

Now let's visit the classroom of Ms. Susan, who teaches down the hall from Ms. Gloria. Ms. Susan has taught in this school for five years. She found the training interesting, and she is curious about how implementing it will work. She feels the pressure and begins the year by setting her testing schedule. Every first week of the month, a volunteer from the university comes to assess the children. Some students are making good progress, and others are not. Ms. Susan sees the need to put the children into small groups to give them more opportunities to practice than they are getting in the large group. To master the skills, some groups need more help than others, so she asks her classroom volunteer to assist. At the fall conference she explains to all the parents that she is going to start sending home a homework sheet each week, so parents can help their children with numbers and letters. Ms. Susan notes that most parents are following through. As the children's assessments are done monthly, she starts to see overall progress. Ms. Susan believes that assessment helps her do her work better.

In this classroom, children are allowed to wiggle during circle time. Dramatic play is part of the integrated thematic curriculum, with the goal of building vocabulary, an important literacy skill. The more children talk, the better. Each center has reading and writing opportunities, so children can make lists or write letters. Ms. Susan wants the children to become familiar with the worksheets they will use in first grade, so occasionally she uses them in her kindergarten class.

Different Kindergarten Styles

The two scenarios described above are playing out, with some variations, in real life. How then should early educators prepare children for kindergarten? It is important for you to be familiar with the personalities of the kindergartens offered in your community, but you should not attempt to prepare children for different teaching styles. Always follow the principles of NAEYC's position on developmentally appropriate practice, and maintain a dialogue with the kindergarten teachers to do a better job of transitioning children and families.

Discussion Starters

- Reflect on your kindergarten experience. What was it like? What did your parents do or say? What did your teacher do or say?

- What do you believe should happen in a kindergarten classroom? How do these beliefs relate to what you have read in this chapter?

- If you were to meet Ms. Gloria, how would you work with her to begin a plan for the transition to kindergarten?

CHAPTER 3

Preparing Children for Kindergarten

It is a beautiful, sunny day in early August. Julia is climbing on the tall jungle gym in the playground of the elementary school she will attend next September. Her mom, Sara, is enjoying a blissful moment of parental pride. As she looks up from her book, Sara watches her daughter using her feet and hands, in perfect co-ordination, to get to the highest platform. Sara feels confident that Julia is ready for kindergarten. Not only is Julia sure-footed on the large-muscle equipment, but the nursery school teacher's observations and the preschool screening results were also very reassuring. They confirmed that Julia has all the skills she needs to go to kindergarten. Julia elegantly goes down the slide, but a second later she is running to her mother, crying.

"What's wrong, honey? Did you hurt yourself?" Sara asks.

Julia is sobbing and stomping her feet. "I don't want to go to kindergarten! I am not going to kindergarten!"

Sara says, "But honey, you were so happy about it this morning. And, look, you love the slide here, and you'll have new friends in kindergarten! And your teacher, Ms. Benson, is really nice. You liked her last week when we visited the school!"

After she calms down, Julia is able to explain why she doesn't want to go to kindergarten anymore. She thinks children should know how to read before they start kindergarten, and she doesn't know how yet. She does not feel ready! She asks her mother to teach her to read quickly. Julia's mom gently reminds her that she does not need to know how to read before kindergarten, because she will learn to read in kindergarten and in the first grade.

Julia's anxiety is normal. Developmentally at this age, children have a good imagination. They can see things in their mind that are not in the present, and what they imagine may cause them concern. Many children are worried about some aspect of kindergarten. It is a new experience, and they are not always sure it will be as great as other people tell them it will be. The checkout clerk at the supermarket, Julia's church pastor, and her great-aunt Phyllis have already asked her several times when and where she is going to kindergarten. It is part of the social rite of passage for five-year-olds to get a lot of attention about the subject, even from strangers. Some days Julia responds with enthusiasm and self-confidence. Other times she feels doubt about her abilities and fears the unknown. Children have many questions in their heads: Will I find the bathroom? I don't know this teacher. Is she going to be mean? Will she be like my Head Start teacher? The school is so big. Who will find me if I get lost? Do we get to play? I'm scared. I don't know the other kids there. I'm going to miss my child care. Why do I need to go to kindergarten?

Going to Kindergarten Is a New Situation

Like Julia, children have a wide range of emotions. Sometimes they are excited to be a big kid, and other times they are afraid they will not measure up, or they have misconceptions about what they should know or do. Those emotions are part of the process of adapting to change. First, there is the letting go of the familiar. Julia will be saying good-bye to her preschool teacher, many of her friends, and the routines of her life so far. Then there is the uncertainty of the unknown. Even though she is getting to know her new school and teacher, Julia still is not sure about *how it is going to work.*

Separation anxiety sometimes appears, even if children have been away from home in child care. During the preschool years, families usually warn children not to talk to strangers. In a new school, many unknown people—from parents of other students to volunteers to other school staff members—interact with children. Children have to make sense of these contradictory messages.

When adults treat these issues with patience, support, and guidance, children can take control of their feelings and actions to make the change in a positive way. They learn the new rules and places, and they get to trust new people. The result is growth and a sense of self-confidence. In addition to providing overall early childhood experiences, caregivers and parents can also work together to plan special transition activities to facilitate the move from home and preschool to kindergarten.

Teachers, child care providers, and families can prepare children for kindergarten. A solid preparation involves being clear about what children should know by the time they start kindergarten. But children also must adapt to their new kindergarten environment.

Temperament

Leo is always ready for a new adventure. He tries new foods easily, and he is the first one to jump on the merry-go-round at the amusement park. Mathew is cautious in new situations. He asks many questions and wants precise answers. When he is interrupted in his play without warning, he protests loudly and shuts down. Different children have different reactions.

Temperament is the way children are. It is part of their natural disposition, informing their reactions to events or situations.

Adaptability is one of the temperamental traits that affects how children adjust to change (Kurcinka 1998). Some children adapt to new situations fast. Others have more difficulty dealing with change. They are slow to adapt, and they react to any new idea, situation, environment, or person in a negative or cautious way. They need more time and careful preparation to get used to a new experience. Since they don't like surprises, they appreciate knowing what the future holds. To help children who are slow to adapt, it is important to take the time to talk with them about what kindergarten will look, smell, and feel like. Who will be there? What will they wear? What will they do? The more details, the better. Visits to the school to meet the teacher, the principal, and the school nurse are good ways to get children used to the idea and help them understand what will happen and how school works.

Before children get to kindergarten, they need closure with their preschool or child care. It is helpful for them to hear how going to kindergarten will change their schedule and routines, whether they are at home full time with a parent or attending a child care program. Playing kindergarten is a good activity for helping children develop adaptability skills, so they can practice their feelings and actions. Reading books about kindergarten and talking about how the characters feel is also a good way to help children process their ideas and clarify misconceptions like the one Julia had about reading in kindergarten.

Intensity is the second temperament trait that influences children's adjustment to a new situation; it affects their response like a "driving force" (Kurcinka 1998). Some children have mild reactions when they are anxious or concerned. They become quiet and get teary-eyed when they are upset. Other children cry, scream, and make a scene. The intense feelings these children have may not be worse, but the behaviors are definitely louder. Obvious intensity can cause more stress on the kindergarten teacher and parents. Parents are embarrassed when their child sobs and pulls at their pant leg at the door of the classroom. Teachers do not have the time to calm down the intense child when they already have a whole group of children to attend to.

What helps intense children? Try techniques such as reading or telling stories, preparing for the intensity by anticipating beforehand how the child will feel, having the child practice more appropriate behaviors, having sensory activities like playdough available to help the child relax, or designating a quiet area in the classroom to allow the child to observe the action before being part of it.

Kindergarten teacher Mr. Benjamin noticed two children who were clinging tightly to their parents during orientation. They would not separate from their parents during story time, and they wanted their parents right with them at the snack table. At the end of the event, when Mr. Benjamin was saying good-bye, he casually made the comment that it is sometimes difficult for children to go to kindergarten on the first day because they don't know what to expect. Then he said, "Boys and girls, when you come next week, the classroom will be exactly the same. We will have the same yellow playdough on the table and the same fish crackers for snack. I will also read the same book I read today. And if you feel kind of sad, although I won't have much time to sit with you, you can stay in the book corner, where it is quiet. You can watch what happens until you are ready to join in." Offering this reassurance was a good strategy to help the intense children who need more support for adaptation!

The third consideration regarding temperament is whether the child is an extrovert or an introvert. Introverts get their energy from being alone, so being in a group with many other children and adults in school can be quite difficult for them. Introverts tend to need time to think before they speak, and they're unlikely to raise their hand easily to volunteer comments. In order to get their space, they may linger quietly in the book or block corner for long periods. Extroverts, on the other hand, get their energy from being with other people. They think aloud and love being the first one to respond to the teacher's questions. They act friendly. The adjustment to school tends to be easier for extroverts, who know how to get attention and connect with others easily. Extroversion is more common and more valued in our society. Introversion is often labeled as shyness and is viewed in a more negative light.

Child Development 101: Growth Is Not a Straight Arrow

In chapter 1, we discussed what the children in this age range can be expected to do. Now I want to draw a brief, typical profile of day-to-day developmental behaviors. You can easily find many developmental checklists in books and on the Internet.

It is important to remember that growth does not happen as a straight upward arrow. It is better to visualize growth as an upward spiral. As you follow the movement of a spiral, it goes up and around, then down and around, and up again. In the down and around stages, children may not look or feel as competent as they did just a few days earlier. This is part of the normal cycle of physical and mental growth that affects other areas. For example, as the eyes develop and the child gets taller, depth perception changes, so a child who has looked very competent going up and down the slide at the park might suddenly freeze at the top, as though he has lost his skills. The reality is that until his body adjusts again the bottom of the slide looks much farther away than it did a few days earlier.

Between the ages of four and six, much learning happens, yet it may seem inconsistent. The pattern of growth with periods of equilibrium and disequilibrium, identified in the twentieth century by Arnold Gesell and his colleagues (Gesell, Halverson, Thompson, Ilg, Castner, Bates Ames, and Amatruda 1940), provides a helpful way to understand children. In addition, other theorists, such as Erikson, Piaget, and Lawrence Kohlberg, have given us a valuable foundation from which to interpret child development. They help us understand what general behaviors to expect and why children think and act in predictable ways. Think of the spiral as you read about development.

Physical Development

On average, children between the ages of three and six grow from two to three inches and gain four to six pounds per year. Sleeping, eating, and elimination patterns are established. Permanent teeth appear. The preference for right- or left-handedness is fixed. In order to grow healthy bodies, children need family and school routines that provide a balanced diet, ten to twelve hours of sleep in a twenty-four hour period, and the opportunity to exercise their large and small muscles.

Brain Development

The brain continues to grow and reaches adult size by the time children are six. The time between birth and six years is a *sensitive* period, during which it is important to provide many opportunities for developing children's intelligence. While it is true that the more stimulation there is, the better the synapses grow and multiply, recent neuroscience research has shown that the brain is more elastic and resilient than we once thought. Children who have not had optimal opportunities to learn at home are not doomed. They can learn in other environments, such as child care and school, and with other adults, such as caregivers and teachers.

Perceptual-Motor Development

Children's perceptual-motor development refers to the ability to move their bodies in relation to other objects they perceive in the environment and to make appropriate accommodations to avoid bumping or over-reaching. At the ages of four and five, perceptual-motor development is still evolving. The length of children's arms and legs continues to change as they grow fast. That means large- and small-motor coordination can be inconsistent. Children may be able to write perfect letters one day and not-so-perfect letters the next day, as their ability to hold a pencil changes. Children will also reverse letters such as *E* and *F* or *b* and *d* as their vision continues to develop.

Social-Emotional Development

Erik Erikson described children in this age group as being in the *initiative vs. guilt* stage. Children have lots of energy, and they forget their failures and mistakes quickly, which is a good thing, because they have a lot to learn, and they will make many mistakes in the process. Their imagination grows with their language and vocabulary. The more words and concepts children have, the more ideas they have in their brains. This leads to fantasies with make-believe stories and tall tales, which in turn can cause guilt and anxieties.

For example, recall earlier in this chapter that Julia imagined she should know how to read before kindergarten. Realizing she was falling short of this self-imposed expectation, she felt anxious. At this stage, if children get the sense from adults that they are bad for their sometimes clumsy attempts and explorations, or if their anxieties are dismissed as trivial, the consequence is a stifling of their sense of initiative. They become afraid to try again. When Julia's mother patiently explains that she won't be required to read in kindergarten and expresses her confidence that Julia *will* learn to read in school, Julia learns that her abilities are in line with her age. Her sense of competence is then restored.

Moral Development

Kohlberg described children of this age group as being in the preconventional stage of reasoning. Their sense of morality is external. They believe in adages such as "might makes right," "survival of the fittest," and "the strongest one wins." They act based on fear of punishment and desire for reward. For example, children stop their negative behavior when they hear adults use the "countdown" technique of classroom management or when they're promised a sticker for good behavior. They may not quite understand the cause and effect, but they want the sticker. When adults help children use language and everyday situations to examine issues of right and wrong, children learn the tools to progress well into the stage of internal morality, an important skill to regulate behavior.

Cognitive Development

Piaget described children of this age group as being in the preoperational stage. In this stage, children construct their own understanding of concepts and operations (cause and effect, classification, logical reasoning) by active exploration with objects and people. This is especially meaningful when children think and reflect about what they are doing. They may not have the language to actually reflect, but when adults give children words and help processing them, children learn to use language to represent, remember, and plan things and events. At this stage children use symbolic play, so they do not have to have the real thing. For example, they use a stick as a gun, or they pretend that a fire needs putting out and use an imaginary hose. Children are egocentric and see the world mostly from their point of view. They are still inefficient in problem solving, but they are always questioning and investigating, so adults can help them think through what they are doing by using open-ended questions and concrete experiences.

Relating Child Development to Kindergarten Readiness

When thinking about children being ready to go to kindergarten, we should consider where the children are on the developmental road. Overall, children of kindergarten age are optimistic little creatures, with lots of energy and a desire to learn. When we pay attention to what they need in their classrooms and homes, we give them the best chance to be ready for school. It is not about *pushing down the curriculum;* rather, kindergarten readiness is about being intentional in providing learning opportunities that are concrete and relevant to children's developmental stage. Readiness is about active exploration that mobilizes their bodies and senses to learn early literacy, math, and social skills. It involves providing excellence in all areas of practice (Copple and Bredekamp 2009).

Preparing Dual-Language Learners

Pablo and Thao, two boys who are both four-and-a-half years old, attend a Head Start program where the instruction is in English. The boys are dual-language learners. Pablo is Latino. His parents are immigrants from Guatemala who arrived six months ago from their mountain village. They speak Spanish at home; they do not speak English. Pablo's parents have a second grade education. Thao is Hmong. His parents speak Hmong and English at home. They came to the United States as refugees ten years ago, when they were in their teens, and they graduated from high school here. Thao was born in the United States. Before entering Head Start, his elderly great-grandparents provided child care for him and his cousins while their parents and grandparents worked. Thao's grandparents speak only Hmong.

On a snowy March day, Pablo and Thao are playing with dinosaurs in the block area. Each is holding a dinosaur, and they are facing each other and roaring. They hold their tyrannosaurus and brontosaurus out and shake them close to each other's face. "Roar, roar, roar!" They smile and are careful not to hurt each other. It is obvious that they like each other and are good buddies. After five minutes, Thao says, "Come, come!" The boys bend down to the floor and begin building a cave for the dinosaurs. To decide on what blocks to use, they show the blocks to each other and nod if they approve or they say, "Come, come." This cooperative play goes on for another fifteen minutes with no language other than the roaring sounds and "Come, come." The teacher comments that these children do so well playing together they do not need her to intervene.

Dual-language learners in the United States are children who speak a language other than English at home and who are learning English at school. In other words, they are learning two languages. There are three types of formal educational opportunities for dual-language learners: programs that offer instruction in their home language, bilingual programs that offer both their home language and English, or programs that offer only English as the language of instruction. These options are possible in preschool as well as in elementary school.

In most cases, dual-language learners attend schools where the language of instruction is English. There are two primary practical reasons for this. First, in most areas of the United States, several languages are represented in the classrooms, so English is the common language for all. The second reason is that the majority of teachers are monolingual English speakers.

Let's think about Pablo and Thao again. Are they ready for kindergarten? They seem to have the social skills to be in kindergarten. Should we be concerned about their language skills? They will be going to an English-language kindergarten. To be ready for kindergarten, dual-language learners need to have the skills to say what they think, feel, want, and need. That means they should be able to do so as much as possible in English if they are going to attend an English-language kindergarten.

At the first national Head Start Dual Language Institute, the best thinkers on this topic shared their research, explaining it is not only possible but also necessary to provide explicit instruction in the dominant language, always in a developmentally appropriate manner, while finding ways to support learners' home languages (Tabors 2008; Espinosa 2007). Children who are dual-language learners need the following:

- explicit instruction in English, with a strong curriculum that is well integrated to learn concepts and vocabulary in English

- teaching that builds on children's knowledge of the world from their home language

- continuity between home and school culture, by helping their parents understand what the children are learning in the classroom

- encouragement for their parents, so children continue to speak the home language at home, build concepts, and maintain their cultural connection

- recognition that their families have the strength and desire for the children to do well in school

- ways to honor and acknowledge their cultural and linguistic heritage

Preparing Children with Special Needs

Marta is six years old. She has Down syndrome. She has been in early childhood special education since she was a baby, first in a home-visiting birth-to-three program, then in a center-based program located in her neighborhood elementary school. Now she is in an inclusion classroom where there are four special education children and eight mainstream education children. The staff includes a preschool teacher and two assistants. A special education specialist comes every day for two hours to provide extra support. Next year Marta is going to an inclusion kindergarten.

Marta is gregarious and makes friends easily. She can write an *M,* and she happily puts *M* on everything she paints or scribbles. Her favorite time of the day is active learning, when she spends her time in the housekeeping corner, cooking and rocking and feeding the dolls. She is learning so much in this nurturing and stimulating early childhood classroom that her parents are very nervous about her move to elementary school. They worry that Marta will not have the same level of support and that her growth will slow down. Her parents' concerns can be alleviated with a good plan. Children who receive special education services need the same consideration and activities as their typically developing peers receive while they transition to kindergarten. Additionally, children with special needs may require the following:

- a coherent plan to avoid overwhelming their parents

- a choice of kindergarten placement to meet legal rights, which may be easier in large school districts than in small ones

- information presented in different forms and repeated over a period of time, to prevent confusion

- inclusion in all transition-to-kindergarten activities and extra support groups that address their parents' special concerns, such as transportation

Understanding the Kindergarten Teacher's Challenges

Empathy breeds positive actions. I believe it is important for early childhood educators to understand the challenges of their colleagues, the kindergarten teachers. So here is a glimpse into their reality. According to kindergarten teachers, about 52 percent of children have a very successful entry to kindergarten, with virtually no problems. Thirty-two percent have a moderately successful entry, with some problems. Sixteen percent have a difficult or very difficult entry, with many problems, or the teacher has serious concerns about the child's academic progress or adjustment to school (Pianta, Rimm-Kaufman, and Cox 1999).

For the first group of children, the minor problems relate to uneasiness in the first few days of adjusting to a new place, people, and routines. The second group experiences problems relating to adjustment and pre-academic preparation. They may know how to share and play with other children, but they may not know how to handle books, listen to a story, or use markers to draw and scribble. The last group, though the smallest, is made up of children whose adjustment is more difficult because they lack the necessary social and pre-academic skills. They may not know how to function in a group setting, have intense separation anxiety, or have a low vocabulary and not know how to express what they want or need. They may be dual-language learners, have special needs that have not been diagnosed, or have a home culture that is so different from the school culture that they feel lost.

Looking at percentages is a neutral way to see the issue. We can tell ourselves that we need to worry about only a relatively small number of children; however, the impression changes if we visualize a real kindergarten class with twenty-two children. Now we can see that eleven children will do just fine, seven children will have moderate needs, and four children will need intensive assistance from their kindergarten teacher. From this perspective, we can better empathize with the challenges kindergarten teachers face. The research certainly makes a convincing argument for paying attention to how we prepare children. It also indicates that the job of preparing children is a shared job.

Whose Job Is It to Prepare Children for Kindergarten?

Parents, pre-K teachers, and kindergarten teachers each have a role in helping children transition to school. A winning formula can be achieved when they consider children's temperamental and developmental characteristics, as well as the expectations of kindergarten. The first step is to be aware of how the children may react. The second step is to prepare some special activities. All the activities listed in this chapter are good for all children. The children who are less adaptable and more intense may need more time and careful preparation.

What the adults do to prepare children for kindergarten makes the biggest difference in their adjustment to school. Both teachers and parents have an important role. Teachers and caregivers can support children directly and through their work with parents.

"Parents are the child's first teachers" is a common phrase used in most documents and discourse from educators. The original intent is to empower parents so they feel equal in their relationship with teachers. The objective is to insure that professionals do not take over the functioning of the family. In practice, however, educators are sometimes tempted to blame parents when they do not act according to professional rules and expectations (Christenson 1999). For example, parents who do not read to their children every night or who do not attend parent-teacher conferences are seen as not caring about their child's education.

Parents are the first teachers for life, and teachers are the first teachers for formal education. This distinction is important to balance the responsibility for getting children ready for school. Using health care—another professional field of great value to families—as an example, we could say that parents are children's first doctors when they notice a hot forehead and the child pulling his ears, take the child's temperature, and correctly diagnose an ear infection. They know something is wrong with their child, and they have the good sense to realize their child needs medical attention. We do not expect them to know the cure.

Parents with a low level of education do not have the same skills to talk, read, and write with their children as those with a high level (Hart and Risley 1995). Parents with a low level of education look to professional educators, who have technical expertise, to teach their children. When these parents say it is the job of the school to teach, it is important to understand and value their perspective. They are already demonstrating a high interest and commitment in education by enrolling their child in a preschool program. Early childhood educators can definitely show parents how reading to children is a good thing. Educators cannot expect that parents will read to their children in the same way and cannot accuse parents of failing their parental responsibility, but they can provide them with all the tools they need to help their child (in the same way the prevention strategies or diagnosis, prescriptions for medicine, and instructions on how to give it would be given in the field of health care). Educators need to take a no-fault attitude in order to partner with parents most effectively (Melton, Limber, and Teague 1999).

The responsibility for preparing children for school is shared between families, preschool personnel, and kindergarten staff. The table that follows helps to conceptualize this balance of responsibilities.

What Children Need to Be Ready for and to Succeed in Kindergarten	*Family Responsibility*	*Preschool Program or Family Child Care Responsibility*	*Kindergarten Responsibility*
Physical health	Shelter, food, clothes, safety, and a healthy lifestyle, including family routines that respect sleep	A safe, clean learning environment Information to families on child growth and development	A safe, clean learning environment
Strong early literacy and language skills	Opportunities for talking and reading in the home language Ongoing learning experiences at home	Language- and literacy-rich curriculum Intentional instruction in English or the home language Ideas for parents to do at home that are related to what children are learning in the classroom	Language- and literacy-rich curriculum Intentional instruction in English or the home language Ideas for parents to do at home that are related to what children are learning in the classroom
Strong social and emotional skills	Love, nurturance, positive discipline	Positive environment Respect for and acknowledgment of diversity	Positive environment Respect for and acknowledgment of diversity
Positive attitude toward learning	A supporting role in children's education Space and time for learning Encouragement of curiosity	High, developmentally appropriate expectations to encourage and challenge children	High, developmentally appropriate expectations to encourage and challenge children Information to families on helping children to be academically successful

What Children Need to Be Ready for and to Succeed in Kindergarten	Family Responsibility	Preschool Program or Family Child Care Responsibility	Kindergarten Responsibility
Special activities to adjust to kindergarten	Talking, reading, and writing related to kindergarten Participation in activities offered by the preschool and kindergarten Completion of the required registration procedures in a timely manner	Talking, reading, and writing related to kindergarten Inclusion of transition activities in the preschool curriculum	Opportunities for learning about kindergarten
Welcome	Support for the children through adjustments to the new school	A positive send-off to kindergarten	A simple process for registering Inclusion of preschool routines and books in the curriculum Welcoming activities: open house, Kinder Kamp, welcome letter Activities provided on a flexible schedule
Families working with the school as partners	Use of positive strategies to collaborate with the school	Training and support for parents to learn how to participate and have meaningful roles	Training and support for parents to learn how to participate and have meaningful roles Activities provided for families on a flexible schedule
Families supported by the community	Knowing where and how to find community resources	Providing access to support services that enhance the formal education of children (health care, cultural events)	Providing access to support services that enhance the formal education of children (health care, cultural events)

Special Transition-to-Kindergarten Activities

Children benefit from specific transition activities that help them prepare for kindergarten. At home, children hear their parents talk about finding a school and registering for kindergarten. In their early childhood classroom or family child care home, children should also have opportunities to talk about kindergarten and play kindergarten so they have an idea of what to expect.

For classrooms and family child care homes with children of mixed ages, toddlers and young preschoolers also will have fun playing school and anticipating what they will do in the near future, because all children will eventually go to kindergarten. Younger children often make willing "students" for the older children, who will read to them, teach them the alphabet, or have fingerplays. If they are not at all interested, younger children will ignore these activities but do the other fun things you have prepared for them. Telling younger children about their older friends who are going to kindergarten helps to prepare them for their own eventual separation, when they no longer attend your program.

A list of fun, meaningful activities for children who are going into kindergarten within a year follows. The activities are arranged by season, starting with winter, which is when official preparation for school begins, and continuing through summer's end. In January, parents begin attending fairs, visiting schools, and making appointments for preschool screenings and physical checkups. They gather immunization records and birth certificates. Children become aware that all of this activity means a change in their life is coming, and it is appropriate for teachers to introduce the topic of coming change with them.

Winter Activities: January, February, and March

- Talk with children about the skills they are learning in your classroom or child care home.

These conversations can be casual or formal. It is important to tell children that what they are doing before they go to kindergarten will be useful in kindergarten. That way they can see how the learning they are doing in their classroom, family child care program, or home relates to going to kindergarten. Here is a simple way to explain the concept: "You will be even smarter in kindergarten," or "You will know how to do it in kindergarten." While this may seem obvious to adults, it is not for children. This knowledge helps them build confidence in themselves as learners and in their abilities to achieve in school. Children's knowledge of their own skills helps them to develop a positive outlook on learning. The skills they are learning include the following:

Learning the names and sounds of letters
Rhyming
Writing letters and their names
Listening to and telling stories
Counting
Singing
Sitting in circle
Finishing puzzles
Building with large and small blocks
Sorting colors and objects
Cutting with scissors
Painting
Gluing
Drawing
Playing and sharing with friends
Talking about what they need, want, and feel
Going to the bathroom
Washing their hands
Dressing and undressing
Keeping track of their things

- Develop a portfolio of each child's work.

  Rather than keeping a portfolio as a teacher-only tool, engage the children in collecting samples, which may include drawings, written numbers and letters, photographs of projects, or dictation examples. Talk with children about how much they are learning and ask them what items they want to add to their portfolio.

- Talk about what is expected and what is not expected in kindergarten.

  Children are expected to sit in circle and listen to storybooks; children are not expected to know how to read. Children are expected to follow their teacher and walk in a line when they go to the lunchroom; children are not expected to find the lunchroom on their own. Having these conversations, which may be conducted in large or small groups, gives children a chance to ask questions and check their assumptions. Like Julia, children may be unnecessarily worried, and they need reassurance. It is important to help children see how the learning they are doing in the classroom, in their family child care program, or at home relates to going to kindergarten.

- Talk about the routines and activities children will do in kindergarten.

  Some routines and activities may be the same as at preschool, and some may be different—playtime; story time; writing; reading; counting; going to the gym, the computer lab, the media center, or the playground; eating in the cafeteria. For children who attend a small family child care, talking about the fact that they will be in school with a big group of children will be helpful. Showing pictures of a kindergarten circle time with twenty children in it will be a good conversation starter.

- Have formal and informal discussions.

  Talk with children about their feelings about change and share your own feelings. Children should have many

opportunities to share their fears and concerns. It is all right
to say you will miss them and that you are also proud they are
growing up and going to kindergarten.

- Write a class book about children's and teachers' feelings about
  going to kindergarten.

  After a formal discussion of their feelings about going to kindergarten, children dictate to the teacher how they feel. They can
  then have their own book and compare it with some of the others
  they are reading. Not only is this a way to teach social-emotional
  skills, but it also is a meaningful literacy experience.

Spring Activities: April and May

- Invite a kindergarten teacher to visit your program and have the
  teacher speak about what happens in kindergarten.

  Sometimes preschool teachers know who the kindergarten
  teachers are in their community, but they may not, especially if
  the school district is large. If this is the case, it may be best for the
  director of the center to take the first step and connect with the
  school or schools in the neighborhood. The visiting kindergarten
  teacher could be a retired teacher who volunteers to visit preschool programs. If you are a family child care provider, contact
  the local resource and referral network office for ideas. There may
  already be established connections with the school district or individual schools, or they may know of a colleague who could be
  a resource. The purpose of this activity is to help children inquire
  about kindergarten. Prepare the children for this visit beforehand
  by introducing the K-W-L format.

- If you have not yet done so, introduce the K-W-L format: what
  we *Know*, what we *Want to know*, and what we have *Learned*.

  This is a complete literacy activity—with talking, reading,
  and writing—that can be implemented in a cycle of five days. For

the sake of convenience, let's assume a Monday through Friday sequence, but any five-day combination will work.

Monday: Tell the children Ms. X, the kindergarten teacher, will visit on Thursday. Show the K-W-L format, separated into three columns on large easel paper. Tell them you will be using the paper to think and learn about kindergarten.

Tuesday: Ask children what they already know about kindergarten. Write their comments in the *Know* column.

Wednesday: Review the list of what children know. Ask them what they want to know about kindergarten. Write their questions in the *Want to know* column. E-mail the lists to the guest kindergarten teacher, if possible.

Thursday: During the kindergarten teacher's visit, read the questions with the children's help. Facilitate the discussion between children and the guest.

Friday: Ask the children what they have learned about kindergarten. Write their answers in the *Learned* column. Make the connection for the children between what they wanted to know and what they have learned.

Leave the chart up for children to refer to on their own or with adult help.

- Have children write a letter about themselves to their kindergarten teacher.

  As the children dictate their words to you, they have to reflect about themselves. This exercise helps them feel proud about themselves as learners, and it helps them process their ideas and feelings about the future. *Dear Ms. ___, My name is ___. These are the things I like to learn about . . . This year, I enjoyed reading . . .* Include drawings.

- Set up a "kindergarten" in the dramatic play area.

  Encourage children to practice being kindergarten students and kindergarten teachers. Ideas for props include books, paper and pencils, stuffed animals and dolls, pointers, an easel with whiteboard, markers, erasers, an alphabet chart, a calendar, school rule posters, name tags, and a poster of bus rules.

- Show a short video of a kindergarten classroom.

  Some school districts have marketing videos you can obtain, or you could ask someone to record students and teachers in action in a local kindergarten classroom. The recording does not need to be of professional quality for the children to enjoy and discuss it. After you've watched the video, talk with the children about what the kindergarten students are doing. Point out similarities and differences between preschool activities and kindergarten activities.

- Read books about kindergarten.

  Some books are about what happens in kindergarten, and many show the mixed emotions of excitement and apprehension that children may identify with. Here are a few books that serve this purpose, and more are available in your local library or bookstore.

  Berenstain Bears Go to School, by Stan and Jan Berenstain. The Berenstain Bears are off to school and have many fun adventures.

  Kindergarten Rocks!, by Katie Davis. Dexter knows all about kindergarten. His big sister has been there already.

  Look Out Kindergarten, Here I Come!, by Nancy Carlson. A family prepares for kindergarten. Henry is excited but also a bit nervous about the new experience.

  Making Friends, by Fred Rogers. Children learn about feelings and making friends.

  My Kindergarten Book, by Angèle S. Passe. Children and parents get ready for kindergarten with this interactive book, with special tips for parents.

When You Go to Kindergarten, by James Howe. Children go
   about their day in a kindergarten class.

- Provide opportunities to review the school's Web site.
    Not only can parents get the information they will need
  by checking out the school's Web site, but they can also turn
  doing so into a literacy activity by viewing it with their children.
  Some sites include a virtual tour of the school. Be aware that
  some families may need to be encouraged to access computers at
  libraries or community centers.

Summer Activities: June, July, and August

- Play in the school playground, which is open to children for
  play outside of school hours and during the summer.
    Children can get used to being on school property. The
  familiarity also gives them a sense of ownership of *their* school.
  When they learn to use the ladders, slides, and tunnels, children
  develop a sense of competence.
- Send children to summer school kindergarten camp during July
  or August, if available.
    As part of their summer school program, some school
  districts offer Kinder Kamps. The length varies from one or two
  days to six weeks. Typically, one or more kindergarten teachers run these kindergarten camps. The teachers get to know
  the children, and the children get a formal introduction to the
  school. They learn the routines of arrival, meals, circle time, free
  play or learning centers, storybook reading, and dismissal. Fees
  and transportation depend on the budget. In some districts, the
  program is at no cost and includes busing. In others, families pay
  a fee and transport their children. If children have a difficult time
  separating, parents may stay with them and gradually leave.

- Attend the school picnic before school opens.

  The week before school starts, or right after, many schools offer picnics with principals, teachers, school secretaries, classroom assistants, and other school staff, including cafeteria workers, nurses, and bus drivers. This is a fun opportunity for parents, children, and school personnel to meet, eat together, and tour the school.

- Attend a kindergarten "play date" before school starts.

  Some schools organize a playground party in August after the class lists are finalized. Children from each class get to know each other and play in the schoolyard.

- Participate in bus safety workshops for children and parents to learn the rules of the bus.

  The workshops often include a presentation by a bus driver or representative of the transportation department, a tour of the bus, and in some cases a short drive around the block. Parents can ask questions about safety and the logistics of the bus schedule.

This list of transition-to-kindergarten activities is quite long, so choose the ones that appeal to you most or those you are not currently doing. The goal is to be intentional in your preparation of the children.

Are Children Ready for Kindergarten?

Children are ready for kindergarten when they have the following developmentally appropriate skills, which allow them to function in school.

They have the language to say what they think, want, feel, and need.
They get along with other children and adults.
They understand their own feelings and the feelings of others.

They have pre-academic knowledge of vocabulary and conversation, phonology, concepts of print, concepts of math, and knowledge of the alphabet and numbers.

They use scribbling, writing, and drawing to represent and interpret ideas.

They see themselves as learners and approach learning with curiosity and interest.

They use their imagination to play and create ideas and objects.

They are well nourished, well rested, clean, and healthy.

They take care of their physical needs (toileting and dressing).

They use school tools (puzzles, scissors, computers, pencils, markers).

They move their body, legs, and arms with coordination.

They transition between activities with ease.

They persist at several tasks throughout the day.

They function well in groups, sharing ideas, toys, materials, and space.

They follow two- and three-step directions.

They sit and participate in circle time and small groups.

They understand they are going to a new school called *kindergarten*.

Discussion Starters

- Think of two children you know and remember how they each react to change. What feelings are the children experiencing? What do their reactions look like? What helps each child cope best?

- Preparing children for kindergarten can be formal or informal. What would be examples of each? What approach do you use in your program?

- When parents send their child to child care or a preschool program, they believe that the program is preparing their child for kindergarten. We know that this is not always the case. What happens in a preschool program that is helping children get ready for kindergarten compared to one that is not? Make two lists and analyze which one your program is in.

- What activities will you do in your program to make children ready for kindergarten? What do you need to implement them? Draft a schedule with three activities you can implement for winter, spring, and summer.

CHAPTER 4

Preparing Families for Kindergarten

Sally is a family child care provider. Emma, the oldest child in her care, is going to kindergarten next year. Since she was a baby, Emma has been with Sally. Sally is sad to see Emma go to kindergarten, but she is proud too. This is the first child graduating from her licensed home, which she started five years ago. When she talks about Emma's parents, however, Sally just shakes her head. "They are just a wreck," she says. "They have a choice of two schools, and they are so nervous about picking the right one. Sometimes they don't sleep at night. They are always asking me questions. What should I tell them? I try to reassure them that Emma will do fine, but . . ."

In the life cycle of families, going to kindergarten is a milestone, just like the birth of a child, five years earlier, and high school graduation, twelve years later. Even if children have been in a child care setting or preschool, this is the first time parents feel they are handing their child over to the big, mysterious institution of education.

When I ask participants in workshops to remember kindergarten, they usually have vivid memories. Sometimes they remember it as a happy time of excitement and discovery, sometimes as a sad feeling of being left in a strange place with people they did not know, being unsure of what to expect. The experience somewhat depends on the person's personality.

Some children adapt more easily than others to new situations; the same goes for parents. Some parents feel confident the elementary school is a good place for their child. Others feel more anxious and uncertain about whether the school will meet the needs of their child.

A Road Map to Kindergarten

What do parents need to know about kindergarten? Maybe we should first ask what parents *want* to know—an important distinction if we are going to be sensitive to their needs. Parents' hopes and concerns are the business of preschool educators who are caring for their children. When we work with the child, we are working with the family too (Keyser 2006). The strength of the caregiver-family partnership is particularly beneficial in facilitating the readiness of children and the transition to kindergarten for all children but especially for those in poverty (Ramey and Ramey 1999; Brooks-Gunn 2008).

In some communities, like large school districts that offer school choices, the entrance to kindergarten can be complicated. Parents are expected to attend school fairs as early as November, visit schools during December and January, and send their preference card to the enrollment office by the middle of February. This means that parents have to be proactive and well-organized, and in many cases, their child has not even turned five yet! With only their own memories of kindergarten and the advice of friends and neighbors, parents do not have a road map to the new kindergarten. Many things in education have changed in the last two or three decades. It has become a more technical field, with professional jargon, rules, and expectations. So even well-educated parents feel anxious.

Parents' Hopes

On the first day of kindergarten, I volunteered to be a community greeter at a school in Minneapolis. My job was to be near the entrance greeting children and parents and directing them to the right classroom if they seemed lost. I saw many beautiful children holding their parents' hands or getting off the bus by themselves. Some had confident steps, and others looked more tentative. All the children were wearing sparkling new clothes and carrying colorful new backpacks. Their parents had probably taken their picture that morning for the family scrapbook.

Six types of school, family, and community involvement have been identified by Joyce Epstein at John Hopkins University: parenting, communicating, volunteering, learning at home, decision making, and collaboration with the community (Epstein et al. 2009). *Parenting* relates to the work that families do to provide for the health and safety of children, as well as to maintain a home environment that encourages learning and good behavior in school. Parenting means making sure children are well fed, rested, and dressed; have good manners; and know how to get along with others.

When parents send children to school in their finery, they want educators to notice they are good parents because they take good care of their children. Parents also hope that if their children look good teachers will have a better impression of their family and will teach their children better. This thinking may be an intuitive response, as the fact is teachers tend to report more adjustment problems among children from families they perceive to be disorganized (Zill 1999).

After more than one hundred years of existence, kindergarten is a normal part of our culture. All parents see kindergarten as the beginning of their children's educational career. Parents *do* want the best for their children, and they can learn how the educational system works.

Parents' Anxieties

As part of a school readiness project in a large urban district, I conducted focus groups with parents to find out what they thought about school readiness, as well as to learn their anxieties and expectations about the entrance to kindergarten.

"Frankly, my biggest fear is the ride in the bus," said Ann, the mother of a four-year-old who was going to kindergarten next year. "You just hear so much bad stuff about the older kids misbehaving and the bus driver not being able to handle it." The thought of leaving a fresh-faced five-year-old on a big school bus with fifty-nine other students, ranging from kindergarteners to eighth graders, is scary, especially when children have to be at the bus stop during hours when it's still dark in the morning.

In addition to bus safety, parents worry about the emotional safety of their children at school. Many questions come to mind: Will the teacher like my child? Will my child make friends? What if my child is bullied? Who will protect him and discipline the bully? Will my child learn things in school that are against our beliefs or religion?

Parents also want to know about the academic expectations of kindergarten, which teacher their child will have, and the placement of their child in a particular classroom. These concerns are practical and have concrete answers that will help parents visualize what their child will be doing and with whom. Having the answers relieves their anxieties and helps parents prepare their children at home for the transition.

Addressing Parents' Feelings and Needs

Parents want to know what to expect. When our daughter entered medical school at the Mayo Medical School, families were invited to an orientation, which started with a welcome dinner to meet faculty and other students and families. The program also featured several workshops that included an overview of the curriculum and course of study, a report on the resources available at the institution to ensure students succeed, and information on what to expect from your student. In this last presentation, family members heard research on the developmental stages and typical behaviors of medical students during their four years of study. In a supportive and lighthearted manner, families were given advice on how to understand the experiences of medical students and recommendations for providing a care package with favorite treats around the time of difficult exams at the end of the first quarter.

While I sat in the audience taking notes, I realized how great it would be to apply this same approach to kindergarten entrance to allay the fears and questions of parents! Not only did I feel confident the school was going to provide adequate preparation for our daughter to become a doctor, but I also could envision my role in the process, even though I am ignorant about the content of medical science. So why not figure out how to do this for kindergarten?

In *Successful Kindergarten Transitions* Robert Pianta and Marcia Kraft-Sayre (2003) report that fewer than half of the families surveyed attended orientation or workshops for parents. When they did participate, however, almost all parents found the transition activity helpful. The major barrier reported by parents was having a work schedule that interfered with the activities offered. Few parents reported choosing not to participate or feeling uncomfortable at school, which negates the myth that parents do not participate because they don't value education or don't like schools.

This research confirms what parents say in focus groups and workshops, which is they want to know more about how to prepare their children. They want opportunities to get to know other families. They want reassurance that the school will provide a quality experience and make sure their student succeeds through timely, regular, respectful, and confidential communication. So let's facilitate this for them.

Families have the right to be involved in their child's education at school in ways that are most important to them. For example, to illustrate what is important to parents, the following is a list drafted by a parent advisory council as a families' bill of rights:

- feeling welcomed at school, with a variety of opportunities for involvement

- receiving timely, regular, respectful, and confidential communication in a variety of formats (in person, written, electronic, video)

- knowing that safety is a priority in school, on the bus, on the playground, and during school-related activities, such as field trips

- receiving culturally sensitive respect from school staff

- being able to access information and decision-making staff who can provide information and solve problems in the school and the district

Helping Parents Prepare Their Children

Immigrant families, families in poverty, and families with low levels of education may not be familiar with the culture of education, and they may not know how to conduct a school search. They expect that the preschool program and school system will guide them to the best options for their children.

In a Hmong parents' focus group, Pheng, a father of five, offered his thoughts. "I want to say that you go about it the wrong way. Your parenting programs' brochures say, 'Come to our program to be a better parent.' But we are already good parents! It should say, 'Come to our program to make your child a better student.'" The other participants laugh, nodding in approval at Pheng's boldness. For emphasis, they repeat, "That is the wrong way! We need to know more about education and how to help our children learn in school, not how to take care of them!" They are right. Now we have to spread this message.

Let's look again at Epstein's types of family involvement, including parenting, communicating, volunteering, learning at home, decision making, and collaboration with the community. These categories, which are commonly adopted by the K-12 system, describe what parents need to know. While educators have focused their efforts on the parenting and learning at home categories, it seems that parents are interested in knowing more about the other types.

Parenting

Parents often need confirmation about how important their job is to the education of their children. We can help them by making the connection between home and school explicit. The following are some examples of how parenting ties into education.

- Taking care of the physical needs of children (food, shelter, and clothing) helps children grow physically healthy and prepares them to learn. When children are rested, they can better attend to what the teacher is teaching. Their brains are more ready to learn.

- Providing the right clothing—such as a coat, boots, and mittens in cold climates—so children can play in the schoolyard safely. With good healthy exercise, children can be better learners when they return to the classroom.

- Teaching children at home about manners, right and wrong, and discipline also helps them to get along with other children and adults in school.

Communicating

Schools have peculiar methods of communication that may not be immediately obvious to families. Teachers should let parents know how their communication methods work.

- The backpack plays a primary role in distributing information. The school newsletter and teacher's notes go home in the child's backpack, and parents need to check it every day.

- Report cards are distributed to families three times a year. They contain information about how children are progressing in school, especially in different subject areas, such as reading and math. The report card also gives parents a sense of their child's behavior. Show parents how to read the information on a report card and what it all means.

- Parent-teacher conferences are typically held in the fall and in the spring. Conferences usually have a set schedule. Teachers often send home (in the backpack) a sign-up sheet for conference times that parents are expected to return. Conferences can last between ten and twenty minutes. If more time is needed, parents may request an additional meeting with the teacher, but, out of respect for parents waiting in line, the meeting cannot usually go over the time scheduled on conference day. You can practice parent-teacher conferences, giving parents tips on what questions to ask and how to be the best advocate for their child.

- Parents need to know that they can contact their child's teacher in person, by written notes or e-mail, or by phone. Teachers are often too busy to have long conversations at drop-off and pick-up times, but these are good times to set future appointments.

Volunteering

Parents are encouraged to volunteer to help the school. The children, staff, and school benefit from the extra assistance. Some volunteer work may be done at school or even at home, such as preparing art materials or making phone calls. At the beginning of the school year, many schools give parents a questionnaire asking them how they would like to volunteer. Even if they don't return the questionnaire, parents need to know they are welcome to volunteer at any time. Some volunteer opportunities include helping the teacher:

- tutor small groups or individual learners in the classroom in subjects including literacy, math, science, or foreign languages
- prepare materials for the art projects or fill backpacks with the weekly news

- supervise a small group of children on field trips
- work in the office, assisting the secretary with making photocopies or preparing mailings
- raise funds for a school project or request donations from businesses
- coach a sport or a club

Learning at Home

Learning at home is an important area to work on with parents so they understand that they can support the job of the school at home with specific actions. Learning at home refers mostly to doing early literacy activities in the course of daily life. Talking and having conversations about everyday events, reading storybooks, telling stories, counting socks while folding the laundry, drawing, and writing are all examples of learning at home. Doing these activities at home reinforces children's learning at school:

- cooking, sewing, painting, and writing letters to relatives all help children become better students by showing them how to apply in everyday life what they're learning in school
- making sure children do the homework assigned by the teacher, including looking for items that start with the same letter, such as, for example, oranges, olives, and oatmeal
- making room at the kitchen table or in a quiet corner for reading and studying
- turning off the TV so there are more opportunities to interact and fewer distractions when children are doing their homework

Decision Making

Families who send their children to a Head Start program tend to have a good understanding of participatory decision making, which is a strong Head Start tradition. Decision making is not as prevalent in private child care centers or in public school readiness programs. Participating in the school leadership council or parent-teacher organizations can be intimidating for parents of children coming into kindergarten. The best way for these parents to learn how decision making works is to be invited to participate by a parent already on a committee.

Collaborating with the Community

Schools have increased the services they provide to families beyond education, including social services, dental clinics, and health checkups for children, and adult education classes, such as language or parenting classes, for parents. The availability of these offerings may not be obvious to families, who will need information to understand how they can benefit.

Six Reassuring Messages

Preparing families for kindergarten requires educators to pay attention to how they explain the culture of their field without assuming parents already know. I see teachers who are discouraged when they plan an elaborate event for parents and few show up. They blame the weather or a lack of parental interest; yet, there are other teachers who consistently have good attendance and response from parents. The message makes a difference. The more direct teachers are, the more they can reach parents effectively. In my work and through conversations with parents over the years, I have found that the following six messages reassure parents as they visualize themselves as partners in education.

MESSAGE 1: Parents and Teachers Will Work Together
to Teach Children

Common literacy-building activities that help children learn at home and at school are talking, reading, writing, and learning new things. The common social skills and behavioral activities are getting along, sharing, respecting each other, learning self-control, and practicing safety.

When parents do activities at home that are similar to what teachers are doing in their classroom, children do better in school. Then the culture of home and the culture of school are in line. In fact, individual families can express their culture in unique ways. For example, literacy activities at home can just as easily involve reading the Bible or the Koran as reading fairy tales or magazines. Talking about what to have for dinner, whether it's tacos or pizza, is useful for the development of children's vocabulary. Once parents understand this concept, they feel validated and supported in the activities they do with their children, which also helps instill in their children the importance of learning. It provides them with concrete examples of true family-school partnership.

MESSAGE 2: Teachers Will Help Children Learn Academic
Subjects at School

When I take my car to mechanics, I expect them to be the experts who will advise me as to what my car needs. On my last visit for routine maintenance, I was given a list of potential preventive actions I could take and asked to choose which ones I wanted. If I chose all of them, the cost would be more than seven hundred dollars! I was totally overwhelmed. When I asked which ones were most important, the mechanic said they were all recommended and it would be my *personal* choice. He kept repeating that he was not forcing me to do anything; he was just giving me the list of my options. I left there confused and irritated. I wondered if this mechanic had just attended a training workshop on car owner involvement. He wanted me to be involved in the maintenance of my own car; however, he was missing a very crucial point: I lacked the information and the confidence to make such decisions. His approach was not helping me.

Sometimes I am afraid we do that with parents. We want them to be involved in their child's academic learning, but we assume they have more background information than they do. When we ask parents to read to their children at home, for example, we may be putting unreasonable demands on them if they cannot read. So when talking with parents about their involvement, we need to first ask them what their ideas are. Then we can reassure them that we will provide the best education we can, because we are the experts in education.

MESSAGE 3: Teachers Will Tell Parents What "Ready for Kindergarten" Means

Parents need to understand what skills children should be learning in preschool in order to be ready for kindergarten. These preschool skills are based on a state's early learning standards. The standards, however, may be too technical for parents to understand without explanation.

The "Are Children Ready for Kindergarten?" list in chapter 3 and in appendix A are more concrete and easier for parents to apply. You can use the list as a guide in your conferences with parents or as a basis for handouts and newsletter articles. (A downloadable version of appendix A is also posted at www.redleafpress.org. Type "ready for kindergarten" in the search box and follow the links.)

MESSAGE 4: Parents Will Need to Help the Kindergarten Teacher Know Their Child

Even though teachers may feel they are not intimidating, many parents report feeling too timid to approach the teacher. In any field, there is a distance between the layperson and the professional, and it is the professional's responsibility to close the gap. Parents need personal encouragement from the preschool staff and invitations from the school staff. Parents can make connections with their child's new teacher by

- visiting the school
- meeting the principal and the teacher
- sharing the child's preschool portfolio
- staying in touch with the teacher with a card or an e-mail whether they are concerned or satisfied

MESSAGE 5: Parents Will Play a Special Role in Helping Their Child Become a Good Student

Kindergarten teachers express concerns that children come to school tired or dressed inappropriately for the weather or an activity. Sometimes their attendance is sporadic. These concerns are legitimate, as they impact the ability of students to pay attention or function well in school. Here are some guidelines for parents, who want to be told explicitly what their role in this area is, to help children become good students:

- When children are well rested and well fed, it is easier for them to concentrate and learn.
- When children have warm clothes during cold weather months, they can go outside for recess and play.
- Children who wear their party clothes to school sometimes worry they will get them dirty. When children wear durable, easy-to-wash clothes, they can do potentially messy activities, such as painting or playing in the sand.
- Children who are in school every day learn more and have better test scores than those whose attendance is sporadic.
- Reading every day helps children become better students.

- Children who watch a lot of TV at home do not do as well in school as those who play and read books.

MESSAGE 6: Kindergarten Will Be a New Experience for All Children

Some children will be excited and happy about going to kindergarten, while other children will be nervous and worried. Some children show excitement on the first day but want to stay home the next day. That's normal. It does not mean the first day was traumatic, only that the novelty of school has already worn off. The transition to kindergarten goes better when parents help children adjust by being sensitive to their concerns and talking about them. Children need gentle encouragement.

Special Transition Activities to Prepare Parents for Kindergarten

At the same time parents are preparing their children for kindergarten, you can take measures to prepare parents for kindergarten. Here is a list of activities to use with the parents of children in your care who are soon going to kindergarten.

- Explain to parents how your classroom activities help children get ready for school.

  How classroom activities help children is not always obvious to parents. As an administrator, I was once called by one of my teachers to observe a parenting group for Hmong parents. The parents had been giggling throughout circle time and would not sing along, which frustrated the teacher. When I arrived, I saw seven moms sitting in a circle with their preschool children, the teacher, and a Hmong interpreter. The teacher started singing "Five Little Ducks." A few seconds into the song, the mothers started giggling, and the teacher looked at me with discouragement. At the end of the session, the teacher and I talked about the purpose of singing "Five Little Ducks." Without hesitation, she told me the children were learning about counting and separation (the baby ducks go out to play away from their mother, who calls them back, one by one). The children were also sitting in a circle, just like they would soon do in kindergarten, and they were learning some English words. It made perfect sense to the teacher that this song had educational value.

Then I asked the teacher if she thought the parents knew the purpose of singing "Five Little Ducks." She was perplexed. Why wouldn't they? Then she smiled, realizing the mothers probably didn't know. The following week, she asked the interpreter to explain to the parents why the song was important. The parents listened attentively, asked questions, and nodded with serious interest when they were told about the song's educational value—and there were no more disruptive giggles. The parents participated eagerly because, of course, they too wanted their children to learn. From then on, the teacher explained the learning objectives of each activity, enriching the parents' understanding.

- Provide parents with good feedback on how their children are learning in your early childhood program.

    Parents want to know not only how their children are behaving, but also which early literacy skills their children are acquiring. This feedback will answer parents' questions about whether their child is ready for kindergarten and will give them confidence in their child's abilities. Parents will then also have appropriate language to describe their child's readiness for kindergarten to the new teacher.

- Teach parents how to use portfolios with the kindergarten teacher.

   Prepare children's portfolios to share with the parents. The portfolio should include assessment results, which demonstrate knowledge of letters, sounds, and numbers. It should also include writing and drawing samples, as well as dictations that explain a drawing or a story. Pictures of the child playing cooperatively in the dramatic play area or showing a structure she created in the block area are also nice to have. These illustrations help parents and kindergarten teachers visualize the child's learning.

- Use parent-child activity books to anticipate the start of kindergarten.

   Consider books such as *My Kindergarten Book* (2005), an interactive book I created for parents and children to talk about themselves and what they will do in kindergarten.

- Offer parent workshops that promote learning activities at home.

   It is important to teach parents, especially those with low educational levels, how to ask their children open-ended questions and to play "what if" games, as well as to encourage parents to talk, read, and write with their children.

- Distribute information to parents about school choices.

   Help parents learn how the process for choosing a school works and how to obtain the deadlines for registration. Often registration materials are written at a high level, which can make them difficult for some parents to read. You may offer to help read the materials, explaining some of the words if need be.

- Encourage parents to attend open houses and orientation sessions at their child's new elementary school.

   Most elementary schools offer open houses and orientation sessions where families are invited to tour the school and meet the staff. Some schools include the children, while others do not. Many of these events are held in the evenings, though some have day and afternoon options. Sometimes families are shy about attending, worried that they will not know anyone, or not understand its purpose as the official welcome to kindergarten. They are more likely to attend if the preschool provider encourages them directly.

- Invite school district representatives to your center or family child care home to discuss kindergarten with parents.

   Parents trust you and will feel reassured about meeting elementary school staff in the familiar setting of your program. Your presence at these workshops is an added bonus, as parents know they can count on you to help clarify information that is confusing.

Education, with its jargon and research findings, is a complicated business for those outside of it. We on the inside tend to forget ever having to learn the meaning of words and concepts like *social-emotional, cognitive, physical development, approaches to learning,* and *early literacy skills,* and we talk without interpreting those terms for noneducators. Jargon can be a problem for parents, and those who aren't used to it can find it confusing or annoying.

A simple glossary of terms and abbreviations frequently used by educators follows. (You may wish to add to the list other terms and abbreviations that are frequently used in your area.) A list such as this one is not only helpful for parents in general, but also is useful for interpreters who have to translate for parents who do not speak English.

I chose a few of the most common terms and acronyms used in early learning standards documents and parent newsletters, and was reminded how unclear we can be in our communication with families. For example, if the teacher says, "Lisa has good social skills," Lisa's dad might smile but leave wondering what the teacher meant. On the other hand, if the teacher says, "Lisa plays well with her classmates, really does a good job of waiting for her turn, and is firm but polite when she asks for what she needs," her dad will have a much better idea of Lisa's "social skills."

Terms

Approaches to learning: how children become curious about learning new things and how they think about what they have learned

Child development: what we know from the areas of child psychology, medicine, and education about how children grow

Cognitive development: how children learn to think, make decisions, and solve problems

Language and literacy development: how children learn to listen, speak, read, and write

Physical and motor development: how children use their growing bodies to make large movements with their legs and arms (gross-motor movements) and to make small movements with their fingers and hands (fine-motor movements); children learn coordination and control of their gross-motor movements when they run, climb, or ride a tricycle; they learn coordination and control of their fine-motor movements when they cut with scissors, use a pencil, or assemble a Lego toy

Self-regulation: how children learn the ability to control their feelings and their bodies so they can behave well; for example, if a child wants to share a toy, the child asks to use it rather than simply grabbing it

Social and emotional development: how children learn about feelings—their own and those of others

Social skills: the abilities that children learn in order to play with others, share, sit in groups, wait their turn, get along with other children and adults, and follow rules

Abbreviations

AYP: Adequate Yearly Progress; schools with low test scores and quality of teaching have to demonstrate yearly that they are making adequate progress toward ensuring all students get a good education; this is the expectation of the No Child Left Behind Act, a public law

BOE: Board of Education; a group of elected officials who oversee the work of a school district

DOE: Department of Education; the U.S. federal government and each state government have a special office that provides guidance and funding for education

ECFE: Early Childhood Family Education; a parenting program available to families with children birth to kindergarten age in Minnesota

ELL: English Language Learner; a student whose first language is not English and who is learning English at school; another term is DLL, or Dual-Language Learner, which acknowledges that a student is learning a home language and English at the same time

FERPA: Family Educational Rights and Privacy Act; the law that ensures the privacy of student records regarding grades and behavior

FTE: Full-Time Equivalent; describes the assignment of school personnel; for example, a kindergarten teacher may teach two half-day sessions as a full-time employee, or 1.0 FTE

IDEA: Individuals with Disabilities Education Act; the law that insures services to children with disabilities throughout the United States; Part C covers children ages birth to two, and Part B covers children ages three to twenty-one years

IEP: Individual Education Plan; a learning plan for children who receive special education services

K-12: Kindergarten through Grade 12; "K-12" describes the school system; increasingly school districts are adopting the term "pre-K-12," demonstrating their commitment to preschool as part of the educational continuum

NCLB: No Child Left Behind Act; a law, the purpose of which is to ensure that all children in every school receive a good education

PTA: Parent Teacher Association; a parent-run board that supports the work of school staff; a school's PTA is a member of the National Parent Teacher Association

PTO: Parent Teacher Organization; a parent-run board that supports the work of school staff; a school PTO operates independently and is not a member of the National Parent Teacher Association

TA: Teaching Assistant; sometimes referred to as EA (Educational Assistant); this employee is a paraprofessional who assists a teacher in the classroom; some kindergarten classrooms have a TA, but most do not

This list of common terms is only a beginning, as there are many more terms that might be used in your area. Make educational jargon more accessible for families by remaining alert and adding words you feel parents should know.

Are Families Ready for Kindergarten?

Families are ready for kindergarten when they can act out their role as partners in the education of their children, which includes doing the following.

They provide opportunities at home for their child to talk, read, and write.

They provide opportunities for their child to experience high-quality group settings.

They follow procedures for preschool screening and school choice.

They choose a school that fits their family's needs.

They complete the registration for kindergarten in a timely manner.

They attend informational events and workshops.

They follow through on referrals to other agencies, such as special education assessment or social services.

They visit schools.

They meet the school's kindergarten teacher and principal.

They attend school orientations and events.

They talk with their child about kindergarten.

They use the information they receive to reassure and prepare their child for the transition to kindergarten.

They develop a plan for being involved in their child's kindergarten and elementary school education.

Appendix B provides a checklist to use as a basis for meetings or as a handout. (A downloadable version of appendix B is also posted at www .redleafpress.org. Type "ready for kindergarten" in the search box and follow the links.)

Discussion Starters

- Think of the families in your child care center or home whose children will be going to kindergarten soon. What are they saying or doing? What does that mean for your work with them?

- Review the list of key messages parents benefit from hearing. Which ones do you feel confident giving to parents? Which ones do you need to practice more?

- What activities will you offer parents to help them and their children be ready for kindergarten? What do you need in order to implement the activities? Draw up a schedule with three ideas you can do for winter, spring, and summer.

CHAPTER 5

Preparing Pre-K Teachers and Child Care Providers

Carmen is Latina and a family child care provider. She has been doing this work for the past ten years. Carmen has a diverse group of children ranging in age from six months to five years. Some children are Latino and speak Spanish at home, and other children are Anglo and are learning Spanish in her care. Through her local resource and referral network, she enrolled in a special early-literacy project that provides her with materials, a rich curriculum, and a literacy coach who visits her every other week. "This has changed my life," she says proudly. "I am much more intentional about what I teach the children because now I know what they need to learn. Before, I didn't!" She enthusiastically names the fun and interesting activities that are integrated with the books she is reading: rhyming, playing restaurant or veterinary clinic in dramatic play, singing and pointing to the alphabet, and playing bingo games with numbers. Now, because she has set up a writing center, Carmen does not worry that children will write on the wall. Her children are more engaged in learning, and as a result, they are also better behaved—quite a bonus for everyone!

Next fall, three of the children—Mona, Luis, and Amy—are going to kindergarten. They are all first-borns, so it is a new experience for their parents, who are quite excited and nervous at the same *time. They love Carmen and are sad to leave her. Carmen is sad, too, but she wants to make sure the children are well prepared for kindergarten. With the help of her coach, she designs a transition-to-kindergarten plan for the children and their families.*

Carmen attended workshops offered by the community school on how to facilitate the transition of children and their families to kindergarten. At the workshops, she learned three things: she has an important role in preparing children for kindergarten; focusing on early literacy and social-emotional skills will help the children become ready for kindergarten; and, for the parents who are new to sending their children to kindergarten, she is a guide to the culture of education. Carmen already knew she was important to the children as the person who cared for them and loved them when their parents were at work. But now she also has a new awareness about the value of her job. She has become more knowledgeable about the expectations of kindergarten so she can teach and prepare the children. She can also work closely with their parents because she has learned about the enrollment and registration procedures in her school district.

Teachers' and Caregivers' Roles

Much of what happens in a preschool classroom, family child care home, or parent-education group serving families with four- and five-year-olds is, of course, preparing them for kindergarten at some level. In my observations over the years, however, that preparation has tended to be rather superficial, providing some general encouragement and individual problem solving but not necessarily offering intentional preparation.

When I talk to groups of early educators, I am always surprised about how many of them have *opinions* about the kindergarten in their community. Then, after they've expressed their opinions, I find out how few have actually visited those classrooms or interacted with the teachers and principals. The teachers make comments, such as "I don't want to talk with parents about kindergarten because I think the kindergartens in our area are so bad," or "When parents ask me for advice, I am afraid to get caught in the middle." These comments make me nervous. I want to propose some actions to encourage and empower early educators to prepare themselves and to work with kindergartens to do a better job of preparing children and families. Kindergarten is their business too.

All Who Care for Children Are Teachers

First, let's clarify who cares for children. From the parents' point of view, anyone who cares for their children has a caring *and* a teaching role. Parents use the word *school* when they talk about child care. According to a 2008 parent survey conducted by the National Association of Child Care Resource and Referral Agencies (NACCRRA), parents have two main goals for child care: a safe, healthy environment and attention to school readiness; however, in a national study of family child care programs, only twenty-four states required family child care homes to have language and literacy materials, and only thirteen states required providers to read to the children. Safety and health are essential to the well-being of children, of course, but I am not addressing that topic within the scope of this book. Rather, I am focusing on the areas of language and literacy that have a direct effect on cognitive and social-emotional development as well as future academic achievement in school. All preschool programs and family child care homes need to follow early learning standards.

Just before Mother's Day, Mona and Luis are at the writing center. On the table, there are envelopes, an assortment of cards of different designs, pencils, and crayons. The children decide to make cards for their moms, following Carmen's earlier suggestion. They are selecting their cards when Amy joins them. Now, all three are busily drawing, writing, and coloring. Mona is writing a succession of unrelated letters. They are well formed and in clusters but do not make words. When she finishes, she looks at her card very pensively for a long time. Finally she shows it to Luis and says, "I don't remember what I wrote. Can you read it to me?" Luis studies the card carefully and replies confidently, "It says, 'I love you, Mommy!'" Amy looks up

from her own work and smiles. "I am writing 'I love you, Mommy'
too!" These three little scholars are getting ready for kindergarten.

This beautiful scene does not happen by accident. It is the product
of an intentional educator. It tells us that provider Carmen is planning
materials and activities to stimulate children's learning so they are ready
for kindergarten. When children grow and learn in a literacy-rich environment, interplay like that among Mona, Luis, and Amy occurs. When
children do not get opportunities to learn, the behaviors that stimulate
their educational growth are missing. The NACCRRA report shows that
learning standards are weak in family child care and strongly recom-
mends that, in order to meet the needs of children and the expectations
of parents, states should regulate higher learning standards in large and
small child care settings. There is no doubt that we need to increase quality if we want to get children ready for kindergarten.

Practical Tools for Gauging Early Literacy Behaviors

Sometimes I worry that we rely on the hope theory of education—we *hope*
they learn! It is a risky attitude when we don't know for sure what we need
to do so children *do* learn. Observing and analyzing our observations is
a good way to gauge if what we hope is happening is indeed happening.
I propose that early childhood educators use two charts to assess the literacy richness of their classroom or home. These charts are not evaluation
instruments. They are tools to develop awareness, and they can be used
for discussion. The first chart (you'll find a template in appendix D and a
downloadable version posted at www.redleafpress.org—type "ready for kindergarten" in the search box and follow the links) is for observing children
in your program and making note of what you see. It is best to use it over a
period of two to three days so there are more occasions in which to see different scenarios and behaviors. You'll record in the "Often," "Sometimes,"
and "Never" columns the initials of the children as you see them doing
the things listed. The second chart (see appendix E for this template or
download it at www.redleafpress.org—type "ready for kindergarten" in the
search box and follow the links) is for making observations of the adults

in your program. Use it in the same manner—for a few days—and in the columns for "Often," "Sometimes," and "Never," write the initials of the teachers as you see them engaging in the practices listed.

Literacy-Richness Assessment #1: *Children's Behaviors*

OBSERVE CHILDREN TALKING, READING, AND WRITING THROUGHOUT THE DAY

In our classroom or child care home, we see . . .	*Often*	*Sometimes*	*Never*
Children talking to each other while playing, while eating, and while transitioning.			
Children talking to the adults, initiating and engaging them in conversation.			
Children responding to adults with language and gestures.			
Children using multiple-word sentences in English, in their home language, or in both.			
Children using computers.			
Children "reading" or looking at picture books independently or with other children.			
Children listening to, understanding, and discussing stories when adults read to them.			
Children scribbling or writing in an age-appropriate manner.			
Children asking questions to gather information and extend their learning.			
Children singing.			
Children listening to and following directions with more than one step from adults.			
Children talking about and drawing their activities and ideas.			
Children dictating their ideas to adults.			
Children counting independently or with other children.			

If you *often* observe children performing these activities, feel confident they are on the road to being ready to learn in kindergarten. If the results are *sometimes* or *never,* then increase those learning opportunities for children. Plan activities that are interesting to the children so they practice more talking, reading, and writing during their time in your care instead of, for example, only at circle time. Remember, children learn best through play and hands-on experiences.

Literacy-Richness Assessment #2: Adults' Behaviors

OBSERVE ADULTS TALKING, READING, AND WRITING WITH THE CHILDREN

In our classroom or child care home, we see . . .	*Often*	*Sometimes*	*Never*
Adults reading to children in a large group.			
Adults reading to individual children or small groups of children.			
Adults engaging children in conversation while reading (dialogic reading).			
Adults asking questions that expand learning and vocabulary (how, what, when, who).			
Adults writing down ideas dictated to them by children.			
Adults listening to children.			
Adults responding to children's questions.			
Adults facilitating play by offering verbal descriptions and suggestions to expand play and vocabulary.			
Adults talking with children during transitions (to the bathroom or cleaning up).			
Adults giving verbal directions.			
Adults promoting conversation during meal times.			

In our classroom or child care home, we see ...

	Often	Sometimes	Never
Adults playing language games (rhyming, making up silly names and sounds, and counting) with children.			
Adults using encouraging words and signs (yes, good, try again, smile, thumbs up).			
Adults leading discussions about stories after reading a book.			
Adults teaching letters and sounds in English and in other languages, as appropriate.			
Adults teaching numbers in English and in other languages, as appropriate.			
English-speaking adults speaking and reading English with children learning English, using gestures as appropriate.			
English-speaking adults teaching English words and sentences to children learning English.			

If you *often* observe yourself and other adults performing these activities, congratulations! You are doing a great job of intentionally promoting language and early literacy skills. If the results are *sometimes* or *never,* be concerned that the early education provided may not be of a consistent quality. Connect with your local CCR&R agency, join your local chapter of NAEYC, or take a class. Often small grants are available for teachers and family child care providers to improve their skills or to buy more teaching materials for the purpose of increasing their quality of work.

Provide Feedback to Parents

Many parents feel they are not getting enough meaningful feedback about their child's learning (Zill 1999). In focus groups, parents say they want to know more about what their children are learning and what they need to learn to be ready for kindergarten. Examples of what early educators say and what parents want and need to hear follow.

What Educators Say	What Parents Want and Need to Hear
Omar is doing so well!	Omar will be ready to learn to read in kindergarten. He has a good vocabulary for his age, and he understands the sounds of English. These are two important pre-reading skills.
Sara likes to play with other children in the housekeeping area.	When Sara plays in the housekeeping area, she shares toys and negotiates with other children. These are good social skills to have in kindergarten.
Michael knows six letters of the alphabet.	Michael knows six letters of the alphabet. To be ready for kindergarten, research says it is better if he knows about fourteen to sixteen letters. We are working on this at school. Here are some ideas to do at home . . .
Mona can write her name.	Mona can write her name. She is ready to do that in kindergarten.
Thao is using more English now.	Thao speaks English with me and the other children to tell us what he wants and how he feels. I know by his answers to my questions that he understands the stories, which will help him get ready for kindergarten.
Marian does not listen well to directions.	We are teaching Marian to listen to directions. In kindergarten, there is only one teacher, so it is important for Marian to learn this skill. I'll tell you what we do at school to help Marian learn to listen better, and let's think about what you can do at home to help as well.

Parents want to know how what their child is doing in preschool will help him or her be successful in kindergarten. Even though children's progress may be obvious for early educators, it is not always so for parents.

Early Childhood Educators Learn about Kindergarten

Early childhood educators develop strong and trusting relationships with parents. Parents often see educators twice a day, and they share intimate stories of life at home. Parents look to educators for guidance in the education of their children. Parents go through their own separation anxiety when their child is moving on to the big next step of kindergarten. Parents may ask questions about kindergarten that the preschool teacher or family child care provider cannot answer if they are unfamiliar with what goes on in kindergarten.

In my work, I often hear pre-K teachers say, "Kindergarten is not my business." Or, I hear teachers say they don't like what is happening in kindergarten, usually implying the schooling is not developmentally appropriate, so they try to avoid the topic. I'd like to encourage you to make it your business to know about the kindergartens in your community. This will help you be more informed, so you can pass information on to parents. It will also help you better understand the system you are preparing children for. If, indeed, you do not agree with what happens in kindergarten, you will be able to advocate for better methods after you are more knowledgeable.

You need to have good information and a connection with kindergarten staff to better prepare children. Here are some suggestions to help you become more knowledgeable about kindergartens in your community.

- Visit one or two schools children might attend. In large cities, children have many more options. If you visit at least a few of them, you will have a better idea of how to choose.

- Spend some time—one hour is enough—in the kindergarten classroom so you can see what children do as well as what is expected of them.

- Attend school district informational events to learn more about kindergarten expectations.

- Become familiar with the registration process so you can guide families through it. You do not have to become an expert, but you need to know where or who to refer them to. Distribute materials about kindergarten registration to families.

- Invite kindergarten teachers and principals to visit your program, and tell them what you do to prepare children and parents for kindergarten. Show them examples of students' work, the parent newsletter, the curriculum, and the daily schedule you follow in teaching children. Kindergarten teachers who understand the educational practices of early childhood see children in a more positive light.

- If your local school district does not have a transition plan, take the initiative. Develop one yourself! Involve school staff. You can advise elementary schools on how to best serve the families you know so well. The next chapter provides information on how to pull the transition plan together.

Are Pre-Kindergarten Teachers, Family Child Care Providers, and Family Educators Ready to Prepare Children for Kindergarten?

Pre-K teachers, family child care providers, and family educators are ready to prepare children for kindergarten when they intentionally include the transition to kindergarten in their curriculum and teaching practices.

They teach intentionally to develop the early literacy and social-emotional skills of all children.

They provide feedback to parents on children's overall development and early literacy skills.

They maintain a consistent portfolio of children's work and duplicate it for parents to share with kindergarten teachers.

They provide early literacy workshops for parents.

They promote home-learning activities.

They invite kindergarten teachers and principals to visit their programs.

They familiarize children with kindergarten classroom rituals.

They stay informed of the expectations of kindergartens in their community.

They visit kindergarten classrooms.

They distribute information about kindergarten to their families.

They support parents through the school choice and registration process.

They train parents to be advocates for their children.

Appendix C provides a checklist to use as a basis for meetings or as a handout. (A downloadable version of appendix C is also posted at www .redleafpress.org. Type "ready for kindergarten" in the search box and follow the links.)

Discussion Starters

- *All who care for children are teachers.* What does this statement mean to you? Think about it. Talk with colleagues about it.

- Use the literacy-richness assessment charts for children's behaviors and for adults' behaviors and assess your home or classroom. What do you see? What needs to change? How will you make these changes?

- What educators say may be different from what parents want and need to hear about their child's learning. Reflect on the words you use when you talk with parents. Can you rephrase your comments to be more specific about how the child's skills or behaviors relate to being ready for kindergarten?

CHAPTER 6

Transition-to-Kindergarten Planning

Mary is a family child care provider. Next year, two of the children in her care are going to kindergarten. She realizes she has not been in a kindergarten classroom since her own children were in school, which is about fifteen years ago. Mary wants to visit a kindergarten and talk with the kindergarten teacher to get ideas about how to prepare the children now. She calls the school to schedule an observation and is pleasantly surprised by the warm reception. There are two half-day sessions, and Mary decides to observe an afternoon session, which is naptime at her child care home. For the hour and a half she is away from home, her husband will be able to stay with the children.

Mary enjoys observing the kindergarten class and is intrigued to see how much writing the children are doing. She takes pictures to show her children what kindergarten looks like. As she leaves, the teacher gives her a handout titled "What Children Should Know before Kindergarten." She also offers Mary her phone number and asks her to call with any questions. Over the next few weeks, the two of them continue to communicate. Mary is grateful for the tips the teacher gives her. She incorporates some of the ideas into her curriculum and shares others with parents. At the next cluster meeting of family child care providers, Mary talks to her colleagues about her experience. They listen with enthusiasm and then ask the local child care resource and referral agency to sponsor a workshop on the transition to kindergarten in order to learn more and do a better job planning for the transition to kindergarten.

Whose responsibility is it to lead the transition-to-kindergarten work? Ideally, the responsibility is shared between the sending preschool program and the receiving school. Someone, however, has to lead. In some places, elementary schools take the lead because they have concerns about the readiness of children coming in. In other communities, preschool programs take the lead because they want to help families feel more comfortable about the transition to kindergarten. Often the leadership comes from an enterprising center director, preschool teacher, principal, or kindergarten teacher who calls a few people and says, "How about getting together to figure out how to make the transition to kindergarten smoother?" What follows are tools for doing just that.

Continuity Is the Goal

The goal of planning the transition to kindergarten is to provide continuity for children and families. Change is stressful. New routines can be confusing. Continuity is reassuring. The more children and parents understand about what will come next, the easier it is for them to put their energy into the new situation. For children, opportunities for continuity include the books they will read in both their pre-K setting and kindergarten, activities they will be provided, and songs they will sing. For families, opportunities for continuity include the paperwork they will be asked to complete, events or routines they will be able to participate in, and services they will be able to access. When preschool and kindergarten teachers and administrators are familiar with each other's settings, they are better able to prepare children and families for change.

Thinking about Logistics

Now that you have a good understanding of what children, families, and staff need, it is time to consider the organizational structure of planning the transition to kindergarten. Organizational structure will vary, based on location. The process and size of the planning project will be different in a large school district than in a small one. The number of people to involve, amount of money to budget, and logistics required to organize it all depend on the specific situation. The planning may be easier to do in a smaller district, compact in geography, where working relationships among professionals have already been established. In larger school districts, it may be more practical for professionals to divide into groups by neighborhood rather than try to cover the entire geographic area.

The most important step is the first one: Start! Begin! Get going! If no one in your community has broached the subject, be the leader! Planning the transition is a necessary service to all families and an especially important one for families who need extra support to understand the educational system. You, as an early childhood professional, can contribute to real systemic change beyond the scope of your child care home, classroom, or center as well as to the overall success of children and families.

Pre-K to K-12 Collaboration

Preschool programs and elementary schools should work together to plan and implement the transition to kindergarten. I often hear teachers say, "Yes, but how do we do it?" It's a puzzling question, since school-readiness programs and kindergarten programs are often part of the same institution. Yet there is a disconnect between them. Part of the challenge is logistical: money is needed to pay for the staff's additional meeting time before or after classes. The other part of the challenge is a difference of perceptions. For elementary schools, there is no urgency to plan for the transition because, ready or not, children and families will show up every year at the appointed time. For preschool programs, however, parents' anxieties over the transition are the incentive to do something to make it easier. I strongly recommend that preschool programs take the initiative to develop a transition-to-kindergarten team. The team's first meeting may be the most challenging to organize; rest assured, it will get easier after that.

A complicated planning process can become overwhelming, so start small and follow a simple framework as you begin. Starting small is okay, and success is more likely later on. Here are the components of a simple process in six easy steps.

1. Convene a transition-to-kindergarten team, involving colleagues from early childhood, elementary schools, and parents.

2. Follow a strategic plan.

3. Choose transition-to-kindergarten activities.

4. Decide on actions needed to implement the transition-to-kindergarten activities, including resources such as money, materials, people, and time.

5. Implement the actions.

6. Evaluate the success of the strategic plan.

Let's begin planning!

1. Convene a transition-to-kindergarten team, involving colleagues from early childhood, elementary schools, and parents.
   Inviting participants is the first step. Connect in person, on the phone, or by e-mail to invite other professionals—pre-K and kindergarten teachers, principals, center directors, family child care providers, family educators, and school secretaries—to a

meeting to discuss the transition to kindergarten. Add parents to the group after an initial meeting, when it is clear the professional team is ready to function. The transition team will probably need to meet four or five times.

Schedule the first meeting on a late afternoon or early evening. Provide a simple meal, such as pizza, fruit, and beverages. If there are no funds for food, participants may be happy to pay for the convenience of a provided meal, or they may bring their own. Make the meeting friendly for people who have been working all day, and allow them to sit down and think in a relaxed atmosphere. Explain the purpose of the meeting, using information from this book as your rationale. Make a plan to invite three or four pre-K parents and kindergarten parents to the subsequent meetings. Ideally, the transition team should consist of eight to ten people, a size that makes facilitating and building relationships more manageable. The last task of this first meeting is to schedule the next meeting.

2. Follow a strategic plan.

The table that follows provides transition-to-kindergarten strategies arranged according to the academic year. With some exceptions, such as in school districts that experiment with year-round schedules, school business is seasonal, with events occurring in a predictable pattern in fall, winter, spring, and summer. Most schools' calendars run from September to June.

Notice that responsibility is shared for some strategies and not for others. Defining responsibility makes the overall implementation of the strategies easier to execute, because each group can focus on the strategy for which it is responsible.

Transition-to-Kindergarten Strategic Plan

Transition-to-Kindergarten Strategy	Responsibility	Schedule
Get staff ready to prepare children and families for kindergarten through training and planning activities.	Pre-K and elementary teachers	Fall Winter
Get families ready for kindergarten through special transition activities.	Pre-K teachers, providers, and parent educators	Winter Spring
Get children ready for kindergarten through instructional learning activities and special transition activities.	Pre-K teachers and providers	Fall Winter Spring
Welcome children and families to kindergarten.	Elementary kindergarten teachers and principals	Spring Summer Fall of kindergarten year

3. Choose transition-to-kindergarten activities.

Once you have your strategic plan to guide you, decide which transition-to-kindergarten activities you want to offer children and families. Review the suggestions for activities to prepare children (in chapter 3), to prepare families (in chapter 4) and to prepare staff (in chapter 5). As you discuss the activities with your colleagues on the transition team, think about transition activities you are already doing and transition activities you would like to add. Start small and choose one or two activities for each strategy.

4. Decide on actions needed to implement the transition-to-kindergarten activities, including resources such as money, materials, people, and time.

After you have chosen the transition-to-kindergarten activities, think carefully about how to make them a reality. The success of your strategic plan will depend on how thoroughly and realistically you realize and manage the resources needed to implement your plan. Good ideas and enthusiasm are not enough! You have to consider the money, environment, people, and materials needed, and the deadlines and leadership required. A blank transition-to-kindergarten action-planning chart is available for your use in appendix F, and a downloadable version is also posted at www.redleafpress.org. Type "ready for kindergarten" in the search box and follow the links.

Example Action Plan for Transition-to-Kindergarten Activities

Transition Strategy	Transition Activity	Actions to Be Taken	Person Responsible	Resources Needed (Money, Space, People, Materials)	Dates
Get children ready for kindergarten.	Set up a "play kindergarten" theme in the preschool room.	Set up kindergarten play in the dramatic play area. Find books about kindergarten at the library. Write a note to parents in the newsletter about the transition to kindergarten.	Preschool teacher and assistant	Books about kindergarten; easel, markers, and a pointer; alphabet chart; dolls and stuffed animals to be "students." No extra money or space are needed.	April 15 to May 9
	End the kindergarten theme with a visit from a kindergarten teacher.	Invite a retired kindergarten teacher to visit the classroom. Prepare children for the visit using K-W-L.	Preschool teacher	Camera Cost: Small gift to thank the kindergarten teacher	May 5
Get families ready for kindergarten.	Provide parent workshops about child development and expectations for kindergarten.	Recruit a speaker from a parent-education program. Reserve the room. Copy handouts.	Center director	Speaker's fees Refreshments cost Meeting room: no cost	January 15

5. Implement the actions.

   Consult your strategic plan as you implement your action plan. You may have to make adjustments if people involved or resources change. Keep in mind the overall goal of making the transition to kindergarten smooth for children and families.

6. Evaluate the success of the strategic plan.

   Evaluate your plan and actions. Take good notes during the implementation and evaluation meetings so you can refer to them when you prepare the transition to kindergarten for the following year. Use the following questions for your evaluation:

   - What aspects went well and why?

   - What aspects need improvement and how can improvement be made?

   - What should we add? What can be eliminated?

Now Is Everybody Ready for Kindergarten?

At a meeting of experts who were designing a professional development system for early childhood educators, the first questions to arise were "Are children ready for school?" and "Are schools ready for children and families?" The discussion was passionate. I understood why the participants were preoccupied with the issues—we must keep addressing the critical and fundamental idea of school readiness. We must continue to pay attention to the readiness of children and the readiness of schools and to look for improvements in both areas. Debating the relative value of each is not necessary. They are both critically important. The goal is to make a strong connection between preschool and elementary education so children, families, and educators have solid continuity.

Play and Learning Standards

While the focus on learning standards is good, beware of wanting to apply standards in a narrow way. In a backlash to laissez-faire free play, in which children interact very little with teachers and there is not much instruction, some preschool educators are choosing worksheets and flash card games at the expense of play (Miller and Almon 2009). Teachers rationalize that they are responding to the mandate to focus on the basics, but this is a faulty rationale, since educational and psychological research shows that in order to get smart, young children need to touch, feel, hear, and talk. We want to see children learn the basics—talking, reading, and writing—*while* they play. Children need time, space, activities, and adult guidance to learn through meaningful, hands-on experiences. When our son, a chemical engineer, was attending college, part of the curriculum included playing with Legos, the purpose of which was to spark creativity and problem-solving skills. All the more reason to expect preschoolers and kindergartners to play with Legos too!

As early childhood teachers and providers, we will have done our jobs—preparing children for school—well only when we remain vigilant about the quality of play in our preschool programs, child care homes, and centers.

Assessments, Teaching, and Learning

Assessing young children is controversial. Inevitably, experts and laypeople have opinions that support or oppose assessment, and each group is a bit suspicious of the other. Can we assess for readiness? Yes, I believe we can and should, using a balanced approach of standardized assessments, parent observations, and teacher observations and evaluations of children's work. If we do all of this, will we still have time to teach? Yes, but it's obvious that a good time-management plan is necessary. Start assessment immediately and continue to assess children's progress at regular intervals. Remember that the most important part of assessment is using the results to help teach children. The early learning standards tell us what children should know. Use assessment to find out if children have the skills to function well in kindergarten, and if they don't, adjust your teaching to ensure they will learn them.

Professional Development

Early childhood care and education is a science and an art. Teacher traits or individual qualities tend to be emphasized more than skills, but I believe skills are more important than talent. Teachers can improve their skills just as doctors can: by ingesting new research and technical information and by *doing*. Look for opportunities to learn more about the transition to kindergarten, early literacy, classroom management, child development, and family involvement. In addition, visit kindergarten classrooms and talk about curriculum with kindergarten teachers as part of your required professional development. If you need to convince an administrator, use ideas from this book for your argument.

Yes, a Good Transition to Kindergarten Can Happen!

There are two wonderful parts to my job: observing children learn and watching early educators teach. In the two anecdotes that follow, the first shows how the quality of instruction helps children learn preacademic skills in a play setting. The second demonstrates how thoughtful transition activities facilitate the adjustment of children to the new experience of entering kindergarten. As you read, reflect on how the early learning standards are applied and how children are getting ready for kindergarten with the support of adults.

CHILDREN LEARNING THROUGH PLAY

In a small rural town on a winter day, it is too cold to play outdoors. The teacher, Ms. J, sees her children are bursting with energy, and, as usual, she dreads letting them loose in the big gym, which her school readiness program shares with the high school. This time, she comes prepared with her "literacy bucket," which contains strips of paper, small notebooks, markers, pencils, tape, stickers, three-by-five index cards, play money, and scissors.

In the gym, she pulls balls, a basketball hoop, tractors, tricycles, and a toy gas pump out of a closet. Immediately, children begin to use the large-motor equipment to tear across the gym at top speed, creating safety chaos. Ms. J sets up three play learning centers—a gas station, a basketball court, and a parking lot near the basketball court. She engages the children in setting speed limits, and they post the signs around the room. Then Ms. J begins to issue fines to the drivers who go above the speed limit. Soon, not only is the traffic madness manageable, but children are also busy buying and selling gasoline, signing checks and using credit cards, making drivers' licenses, counting money, reading signs, and keeping track of the basketball scores.

KINDERGARTEN IS OKAY

Clara is not so sure she wants to go to kindergarten next year. So much talk about it is making her nervous. She does not like new situations. When Jeanine, her family child care provider, sets up a kindergarten classroom in her basement dramatic play area, Clara ignores it for a whole week. Jeanine and Clara's parents know Clara's temperament well, so they slowly present her with stories, comments, and opportunities to get used to the idea of kindergarten. Eventually, Clara begins to play kindergarten, as the teacher to the stuffed animals. Sometimes she is mean and yells at them, especially when they don't seem to follow her directions. Other times, she is sweet and sensitive, imitating her provider's nurturing style.

Jeanine teaches Clara preliteracy skills. They read interesting books, have extended conversations, sing rhyming songs, write letters, and paint. There is a lot of time for play. With her parents, Clara visits the new school, climbs on the school playground, and attends kindergarten roundup. Since she is the only four-year-old in Jeanine's small family child care home, her parents sign her up for the three-week Kinder Kamp in July that is offered by the school. At Kinder Kamp, Clara learns about being part of a large group of children and practices the kindergarten routines.

On the first day of kindergarten, Clara clings tightly to her mother at first. She slowly lets go to participate in the classroom activities. When her mother picks her up and asks her about her day, Clara smiles and says quietly, "Kindergarten is okay."

Everyone Benefits

We can clearly answer the question "Is everybody ready for kindergarten?" when we understand that "everybody" does not apply to just children. Kindergarten is everybody's business: children, parents, early childhood professionals, and elementary school teachers and principals. When adults understand each other and work together, they do a better job of helping children adjust to school, and children have better early literacy and are better prepared for reading. Children also have stronger social-emotional skills, allowing them to get along with other children and adults, as well as to succeed in the social group setting of school. When everyone is ready, everyone benefits.

A Few Last Words

Over the years, I have talked to many early childhood educators, parents, children, kindergarten teachers, and school principals and have discovered a good thing: the transition to kindergarten is smooth for many children and families, thanks to the efforts of countless education professionals around the country. I hope this book has helped you to confirm that the work you already do to prepare children and families is on the right track. I also hope that you feel confident to continue your good work and that your creativity is sparked with new ideas for your program to make your job easier.

We know that about half of children today are doing well in their adjustment to school. Now we need to make sure the other half does well too. In the short term, we need to take a practical approach to getting children ready for kindergarten. Simple activities performed regularly will lead to more complex systemic changes over time.

Over the long term, we must remain alert to our practices: it is imperative that excellent developmentally and culturally appropriate practices are always used in the teaching of all children and in the welcoming of all families. We can accomplish this together by being the best pre-K educators we can and by collaborating with our K-12 colleagues. Together, we can make sure everybody is ready for kindergarten.

Discussion Starters

- Review the steps for planning the transition to kindergarten. Which steps have you already started? What would you need to do next?

- What are the barriers to collaborating with elementary schools in your community? What are the opportunities? Make a list of each. How can you use the opportunities to overcome some of the barriers?

- Now that you have finished this book, review chapters three, four, five, and six, and make notes of the areas in which you are already doing well. Examine the areas in which you would like to put more effort to improve the transition to kindergarten.

Are Children Ready for Kindergarten? Checklist

Children are ready for kindergarten when they have the following developmentally appropriate skills, which allow them to function in school.

- ☐ They have the language to say what they think, want, feel, and need.
- ☐ They get along with other children and adults.
- ☐ They understand their own feelings and the feelings of others.
- ☐ They have pre-academic knowledge of vocabulary and conversation, phonology, concepts of print, concepts of math, and knowledge of the alphabet and numbers.
- ☐ They use scribbling, writing, and drawing to represent and interpret ideas.
- ☐ They see themselves as learners and approach learning with curiosity and interest.
- ☐ They use their imagination to play and create ideas and objects.
- ☐ They are well nourished, well rested, clean, and healthy.
- ☐ They take care of their physical needs (toileting and dressing).
- ☐ They use school tools (puzzles, scissors, computers, pencils, markers).
- ☐ They move their body, legs, and arms with coordination.
- ☐ They transition between activities with ease.
- ☐ They persist at several tasks throughout the day.
- ☐ They function well in groups, sharing ideas, toys, materials, and space.
- ☐ They follow two- and three-step directions.
- ☐ They sit and participate in circle time and small groups.
- ☐ They understand they are going to a new school called *kindergarten*.

Are Families Ready for Kindergarten? Checklist

Families are ready for kindergarten when they can act out their role as partners in the education of their children, which includes doing the following.

☐ They provide opportunities at home for their child to talk, read, and write.

☐ They provide opportunities for their child to experience high-quality group settings.

☐ They follow procedures for preschool screening and school choice.

☐ They choose a school that fits their family's needs.

☐ They complete the registration for kindergarten in a timely manner.

☐ They attend informational events and workshops.

☐ They follow through on referrals to other agencies, such as special education assessment or social services.

☐ They visit schools.

☐ They meet the school's kindergarten teacher and principal.

☐ They attend school orientations and events.

☐ They talk with their child about kindergarten.

☐ They use the information they receive to reassure and prepare their child for the transition from home and preschool to kindergarten.

☐ They begin to develop a plan for being involved in their child's kindergarten and elementary school education.

Are Prekindergarten Teachers, Family Child Care Providers, and Family Educators Ready to Prepare Children for Kindergarten? Checklist

Pre-K teachers, family child care providers, and family educators are ready to prepare children for kindergarten when they intentionally include the transition to kindergarten in their curriculum and teaching practices.

☐ They teach intentionally to develop the early literacy and social-emotional skills of all children.

☐ They provide feedback to parents on children's overall development and early literacy skills.

☐ They maintain a consistent portfolio of children's work and duplicate it for parents to share with kindergarten teachers.

☐ They provide early literacy workshops for parents.

☐ They promote home-learning activities.

☐ They invite kindergarten teachers and principals to visit their programs.

☐ They familiarize children with kindergarten classroom rituals.

☐ They stay informed of the expectations of kindergartens in their community.

☐ They visit kindergarten classrooms.

☐ They distribute information about kindergarten to their families.

☐ They support parents through the school choice and registration process.

☐ They train parents to be advocates for their children.

Literacy-Richness Assessment #1: Children's Behaviors

OBSERVE CHILDREN TALKING, READING, AND WRITING THROUGHOUT THE DAY

In our classroom or child care home, we see . . .	Often	Sometimes	Never
Children talking to each other while playing, while eating, and while transitioning.			
Children talking to the adults, initiating and engaging them in conversation.			
Children responding to adults with language and gestures.			
Children using multiple-word sentences in English, in their home language, or in both.			
Children using computers.			
Children "reading" or looking at picture books independently or with other children.			
Children listening to, understanding, and discussing stories when adults read to them.			
Children scribbling or writing in an age-appropriate manner.			
Children asking questions to gather information and extend their learning.			
Children singing.			
Children listening to and following directions with more than one step from adults.			
Children talking about and drawing their activities and ideas.			
Children dictating their ideas to adults.			
Children counting independently or with other children.			

Literacy-Richness Assessment #2: Adults' Behaviors

OBSERVE ADULTS TALKING, READING, AND WRITING WITH THE CHILDREN

In our classroom or child care home, we see . . .	Often	Sometimes	Never
Adults reading to children in a large group.			
Adults reading to individual children or small groups of children.			
Adults engaging children in conversation while reading (dialogic reading).			
Adults asking questions that expand learning and vocabulary (how, what, when, who).			
Adults writing down ideas dictated to them by children.			
Adults listening to children.			
Adults responding to children's questions.			
Adults facilitating play by offering verbal descriptions and suggestions to expand play and vocabulary.			
Adults talking with children during transitions (to the bathroom or cleaning up).			
Adults giving verbal directions.			
Adults promoting conversation during meal times.			
Adults playing language games (rhyming, making up silly names and sounds, and counting) with children.			
Adults using encouraging words and signs (yes, good, try again, smile, thumbs up).			

In our classroom or child care home, we see . . .	Often	Sometimes	Never
Adults leading discussions about stories after reading a book.			
Adults teaching letters and sounds in English and in other languages, as appropriate.			
Adults teaching numbers in English and in other languages, as appropriate.			
English-speaking adults speaking and reading English with children learning English, using gestures as appropriate.			
English-speaking adults teaching English words and sentences to children learning English.			

From *Is Everybody Ready for Kindergarten?* by Angèle Sancho Passe, © 2010.
Redleaf Press grants permission to photocopy this page for classroom and child care home use.

Action Plan for Transition-to-Kindergarten Activities Template

Transition Strategy	Transition Activity	Actions to Be Taken	Person Responsible	Resources Needed (Money, Space, People, Materials)	Dates

From *Is Everybody Ready for Kindergarten?* by Angèle Sancho Passe, © 2010.
Redleaf Press grants permission to photocopy this page for classroom and child care home use.

Online Resources

The following online resources may be helpful as you look for ideas, examples, and research related to the transition to kindergarten.

Association for Childhood Education International (ACEI)
www.acei.org

> ACEI is a membership organization started in 1892 by kindergarten educators. Its mission is "to promote and support in the global community the optimal education and development of children, from birth through early adolescence, and to influence the professional growth of educators and the efforts of others who are committed to the needs of children in a changing society."

Council of Chief State School Officers (CCSSO)
www.ccsso.org

> The CCSSO interprets "school readiness" as the job of schools to be ready for children and families. The Ready Schools e-newsletter provides information, ideas, and resources to support schools as they work to improve their own readiness. Examples are given for the state and local levels.

Early Childhood Learning and Knowledge Center—Head Start
http://eclkc.ohs.acf.hhs.gov

> The Office of Head Start Web site offers information and tips for parents, staff, and administrators on all aspects of early childhood education, including the transition to kindergarten. Handouts can be duplicated to give to families or to train staff.

Early Childhood Research and Practice (ECRP)
http://ecrp.uiuc.edu

> ECRP is a peer-reviewed bilingual electronic journal published biannually and sponsored by the Early Childhood and Parenting (ECAP) Collaborative at the University of Illinois at Urbana-Champaign. It covers topics related to the development, care, and education of children from birth to approximately age eight. It contains articles on teaching, parent involvement, and educational policy.

Illinois Early Learning Project
www.illinoisearlylearning.org

> The Illinois Early Learning Project Web site has information on early care and education for parents, caregivers, and teachers of young children in Illinois. The resources are relevant to all who are interested in early childhood issues. The Web site offers printable tip sheets for caregivers and parents in English, Spanish, and Polish.

National Association for the Education of Young Children (NAEYC)
www.naeyc.org

> NAEYC has about 90,000 members in 300 local, state, and regional affiliates. Its mission is to improve the well-being of all young children from birth through age eight by improving the quality of early childhood programs, teachers, and caregivers adhering to developmentally appropriate practice (DAP). The organization sponsors and produces professional development conferences and educational materials, including position statements on major issues such as early literacy and assessment. NAEYC offers an accreditation process for early childhood programs and higher education institutions that train early educators.

National Child Care Information and Technical Assistance Center
  (NCCIC)
www.nccic.org

> NCCIC, a service of the Child Care Bureau, is a national clearinghouse
> and technical assistance center that provides child care information
> resources and technical assistance. The Web site has an extensive li-
> brary and provides a wide spectrum of topics, including educational
> content ranging from literacy and child development to child care
> licensing and funding.

National Institute for Early Education Research (NIEER)
www.nieer.org.

> NIEER conducts and communicates research to support high-quality,
> effective early childhood education for all young children. The Web
> site offers practical information and reports on a wide range of edu-
> cation and policy topics. It also provides access to other national and
> international resources.

National Kindergarten Alliance
http://www.nkateach.org

> The National Kindergarten Alliance is a member organization specif-
> ically dedicated to the needs of kindergarten teachers, children, and
> families. The Web site provides information and research on kinder-
> garten education.

United Nations Educational, Scientific, and Cultural Organization
  (UNESCO)
www.unesco.org

> UNESCO is the educational, scientific, and cultural branch of the
> United Nations. It focuses on the rights of young children to care,
> education, and health at the policy level. By the year 2015, UNESCO
> hopes to have expanded and improved early care and education,

especially for the most vulnerable and disadvantaged children of the world. This Web site provides an international global perspective.

World Association of Early Childhood Educators (WAECE)
www.waece.org

WAECE is an international association of early educators based in Spain that is dedicated to innovation in the field of early childhood education worldwide, with a special interest in early literacy. The Web site is available in multiple languages.

REFERENCES

Barnett, W. Steven, Jason T. Hustedt, Allison H. Friedman, Judi Stevenson Boyd, and Pat Ainsworth. 2007. *The state of preschool 2007: State preschool yearbook.* http://nieer.org/yearbook2007. New Brunswick: National Institute for Early Education Research.

Barnett, W. Steven, Dale J. Epstein, Jason T. Hustedt, Allison H. Friedman, Judi Stevenson Boyd, and Jason T. Hustedt. 2008. *The state of preschool 2008: State preschool yearbook.* http://nieer.org/yearbook2008.

Bowman, Barbara T. 1999. Kindergarten practices with children from low-income families. In *The transition to kindergarten,* eds. Robert C. Pianta and Martha J. Cox, 281–304. Baltimore: Paul H. Brookes Publishing Co.

———. 2006. Standards: At the heart of educational equity. *Young Children* 61 (5): 42–48.

Brooks-Gunn, Jeanne. 2008. Reducing racial and social class gaps in school readiness: What we know and what we need to learn. Lecture presented at the McEvoy Lecture Series on Early Childhood and Public Policy at the University of Minnesota, Minneapolis.

Brooks-Gunn, Jeanne, Cecilia Elena Rouse, and Sara McLanahan. 2007. Racial and ethnic gaps in school readiness. In *School readiness and the transition to kindergarten in the era of accountability,* eds. Robert C. Pianta, Martha J. Cox, and Kyle L. Snow. Baltimore: Paul H. Brookes Publishing Co.

Christenson, Sandra L. 1999. Families and schools: Rights, responsibilities, resources, and relationships. In *The transition to kindergarten,* eds. Robert C. Pianta and Martha J. Cox, 143–77. Baltimore: Paul H. Brookes Publishing Co.

Copple, Carol. 2003. *A world of difference: Readings on teaching young children in a diverse society.* Washington DC: National Association for the Education of Young Children.

Copple, Carol, and Sue Bredekamp. 2009. *Developmentally appropriate practice in early childhood programs: Serving children from birth through age 8.* Washington DC: National Association for the Education of Young Children.

Delpit, Lisa. 1995. *Other people's children: Cultural conflict in the classroom.* New York: The New Press.

Doucet, Fabienne, and Jonathan Tudge. 2007. Co-constructing the transition to school: Reframing the novice versus expert roles of children, parents, and teachers from a cultural perspective. In *School readiness and the transition to kindergarten in the era of accountability*, eds. Robert C. Pianta, Martha J. Cox, and Kyle L. Snow, 307–28. Baltimore: Paul H. Brookes Publishing Co.

Epstein, Joyce L., Mavis G. Sanders, Steven B. Sheldon, Beth S. Simon, Karen Clark Salinas, Natalie Rodriquez Jansorn, Frances L. Van Voorhis, Cecelia S. Martin, Brenda G. Thomas, Marsha D. Greenfeld, Darcy J. Hutchins, and Kenyatta J. Williams. 2009. *School, family, and community partnerships: Your handbook for action*. 3rd ed. Thousand Oaks, CA: Corwin Press.

Espinosa, Linda M. 2007. English-language learners as they enter school. In *School readiness and the transition to kindergarten in the era of accountability*, eds. Robert C. Pianta, Martha J. Cox, and Kyle L. Snow, 175–96. Baltimore: Paul H. Brookes Publishing Co.

Gesell, Arnold, Henry M. Halverson, Helen Thompson, Frances L. Ilg, Burton M. Castner, Louise Bates Ames, and Catherine S. Amatruda. 1940. *The first five years of life: A guide to the study of the preschool child, from the Yale Clinic of Child Development*. New York: Harper & Brothers.

Hamre, Bridget K., and Robert C. Pianta. 2007. Learning opportunities in preschool and early elementary school. In *School readiness and the transition to kindergarten in the era of accountability*, eds. Robert C. Pianta, Martha J. Cox, and Kyle L. Snow. 49–84. Baltimore: Paul H. Brookes Publishing Co.

Hart, Betty, and Todd R. Risley. 1995. *Meaningful differences in the everyday experience of young American children*. Baltimore: Paul H. Brookes Publishing Co.

———. 1999. *The social world of children learning to talk*. Baltimore: Paul H. Brookes Publishing Co.

Hernandez, Donald J., Nancy A. Denton, and Suzanne E. Macartney. 2007. Demographic trends and the transition years. In *School readiness and the transition to kindergarten in the era of accountability*, eds. Robert C. Pianta, Martha J. Cox, and Kyle L. Snow. Baltimore: Paul H. Brookes Publishing Co.

Hussar, William J., and Tabitha M. Bailey. 2009. *Projections of education statistics to 2018* (NCES 2009-062). Washington DC: National Center for Education Statistics, Institute of Education Sciences, U.S. Department of Education.

Improving Head Start for School Readiness Act of 2007. Public Law 110-134.

The Individuals with Disabilities Education Improvement Act of 2004. Public Law 108-446 and 632,118. Stat. 2744. Part C, early intervention and Part B, preschool education (IDEA 2004).

Keyser, Janis. 2006. *From parents to partners: Building a family-centered early childhood program*. St. Paul: Redleaf Press.

Kurcinka, Mary. 1998. *Raising your spirited child: A guide for parents whose child is more intense, sensitive, perceptive, persistent, energetic.* New York: HarperPerennial.

McAfee, Oralie, Deborah J. Leong, and Elena Bodrova. 2004. *Basics of assessment: A primer for early childhood educators.* Washington DC: National Association for the Education of Young Children.

Meisels, Samuel J. 1999. Assessing readiness. In *The transition to kindergarten,* eds. Robert C. Pianta and Martha J. Cox. Baltimore: Paul H. Brookes Publishing Co.

Melton, Gary B., Susan P. Limber, and Terri L. Teague. 1999. Changing schools for changing families. In *The transition to kindergarten,* eds. Robert C. Pianta and Martha J. Cox, 3–12. Baltimore: Paul H. Brookes Publishing Co.

Miller, Edward, and Joan Almon. 2009. *Crisis in the kindergarten: Why children need to play in school.* College Park, MD: Alliance for Childhood.

Minnesota Department of Education. March 2008. Minnesota school readiness study: Developmental assessment at kindergarten entrance, fall 2007. http://education.state.mn.us/mdeprod/groups/Communications/documents/Publication/034046.pdf.

Minnesota Department of Education, and Minnesota Department of Human Services. 2005. *Early Childhood Indicators of Progress: Minnesota's Early Learning Standards.* Roseville, MN: Minnesota Department of Education, Early Learning Services.

Mooney, Carol Garhart. 2000. *Theories of childhood: An introduction to Dewey, Montessori, Erikson, Piaget, and Vygotsky.* St. Paul: Redleaf Press.

National Association of Child Care Resource and Referral Agencies (NACCRRA). 2008. *Leaving children to chance: NACCRRA's ranking of state standards and oversight of small family child care homes.* Arlington, VA: NACCRRA.

National Center for Education Statistics (NCES). 1993. *Public school kindergarten teachers' views on children's readiness for school.* Washington DC: U.S. Department of Education, Office of Educational Research and Improvement, and National Center for Education Statistics.

Neuman, Susan B., Carol Copple, and Sue Bredekamp. 1999. *Learning to read and write: Developmentally appropriate practices for young children.* Washington DC: National Association for the Education of Young Children.

No Child Left Behind Act of 2001. Public Law 107-110, 115. Stat. 1425, enacted January 8, 2002.

Olson, Lynn. 2007. Improving children's chances. In *From cradle to career: Connecting American education from birth through adulthood,* 10-31. Bethesda, MD: Editorial Projects in Education Research Center.

Passe, Angèle. 1994. A model for training family educators in multiculturalism. Master's thesis, University of Minnesota.

———. 2005. *My kindergarten book*. Minneapolis: Literacy Press International.

Pianta, Robert C. 2007. Early education in transition. In *School readiness and the transition to kindergarten in the era of accountability*, eds. Robert C. Pianta, Martha J. Cox, and Kyle L. Snow, 3–10. Baltimore: Paul H. Brookes Publishing Co.

Pianta, Robert C., and Marcia Kraft-Sayre. 2003. *Successful kindergarten transition: Your guide to connecting children, families, and schools*. Baltimore: Paul H. Brookes Publishing Co.

Pianta, Robert C., Sara E. Rimm-Kaufman, and Martha J. Cox. 1999. Introduction: An ecological approach to kindergarten transition. In *The transition to kindergarten*, eds. Robert C. Pianta and Martha J. Cox, 3–12. Baltimore: Paul H. Brookes Publishing Co.

Ramey, Craig T., and Sharon L. Ramey. 1999. Beginning school for children at risk. In *The transition to kindergarten*, eds. Robert C. Pianta and Martha J. Cox, 217–52. Baltimore: Paul H. Brookes Publishing Co.

Shore, Rima. 1998. *Ready schools: A report of the goal 1 ready schools resource group*. Washington, DC: The National Education Goals Panel.

Slate, Joseph, and Ashley Wolff. 1996. *Miss Bindergarten gets ready for kindergarten*. New York: Puffin Books.

Snow, Catherine E., M. Susan Burns, and Peg Griffin, eds. 1998. *Preventing reading difficulties in young children*. Washington DC: National Academy Press.

Tabors, Patton O. 2008. *One child, two languages: A guide for early childhood educators of children learning English as a second language*. 2nd ed. Baltimore: Paul H. Brookes Publishing Co.

Tabors, Patton O., Diane E. Beals, and Zehava O. Weizman. 2001. "You know what oxygen is?": Learning new words at home. In *Beginning literacy with language: Young children learning at home and school*, eds. David K. Dickinson and Patton O. Tabors. Baltimore: Paul H. Brookes Publishing Co.

Villegas, Anna María, and Tamara Lucas. 2002. *Educating culturally responsive teachers: A coherent approach*. Albany: State University of New York Press.

West, Jerry, Kristin Denton, and Lizabeth M. Reaney. 2000. *The kindergarten year: Findings from the early childhood longitudinal study, kindergarten class of 1998–99*. Washington, DC: Education Statistics Services Institute.

Zill, Nicholas. 1999. Promoting educational equity and excellence in kindergarten. In *The transition to kindergarten*, eds. Robert C. Pianta and Martha J. Cox, 67–105. Baltimore: Paul H. Brookes Publishing Co.